Collins

English Expert

COURSEBOOK 6

Name: ....

Grade: .... Section: ....

Look at the two pictures.
When joined together, they form a compound word.

What is the word?

....

Kashmira Jaiswal | Radhika Tadepalli | Somali Mitra

HarperCollins*Publishers*

Publishing operations in 17 countries and 120+ imprints globally

William Collins' dream of knowledge for all began with the publication of his first book in 1819. A self-educated mill worker, he not only enriched millions of lives, but also founded a flourishing publishing house. Today, staying true to this spirit, Collins books are packed with inspiration, innovation and practical expertise. They place you at the centre of a world of possibility and give you exactly what you need to explore it.

Published by Collins Learning
An imprint of HarperCollins*Publishers* India
Building No. 10, Tower A, 4th Floor, DLF Cyber City, Gurugram, Haryana 122002, India

First edition: 2024
Reprint edition: 2025
ISBN: 978-93-6213-265-9

The publishers would like to thank the following reviewers for their suggestions and inputs:

Renu Arora
Head of the Department, English
Saint Margaret Senior Secondary School, New Delhi

Shalini Sharma
Mother's International School

Radhika Tadepalli
Principal,
Modern Academy Senior Secondary School, Ghaziabad
Printed and bound by Thomson Press India Ltd

Browse the complete Collins catalogue at www.collins.in.
For any queries/feedback, please write to us at SCHOOLSUPPORT@harpercollins.co.in.

English Expert is a new multi-skill course in English that aims to address the needs of the learners, as underlined in the National Curriculum Framework (NCF) 2023, one of whose underlying principles is a concerted shift towards competency-based learning. This series is distinct in its inclusion of curricular goals, mapped to the respective competencies outlined by the new NCF. It focuses on literacy through thoughtfully curated content, exercises, and activities that will help to develop the 3Hs – Curious Heads, Skilled Hands, and Compassionate Hearts.

Grades 1, 3, and 6 include bridge chapters that act as a pedagogical link between the Foundational, Middle, and the Preparatory Stages. The formal requirements of language are integrated with the appreciation of literature-rich content. This is done through a combination of the communicative and the language-through-literature approaches towards language acquisition.

Care has been taken to include India-focused content and activities adhering to the principles of experiential learning and mindfulness. Additionally, the series aims to develop 21st century skills and awareness about the United Nations' Sustainable Development Goals in learners. It also fosters art integration through activities.

Coursebooks 1–8 comprise a mix of prose, poetry, and drama authored by Indian and global writers, based on themes like self and family, climate change, gender, and inclusivity. The exercises include factual, analytical, life skills, and value-based questions. Grades 6–8 include a HOTS-based comprehension section, in keeping with the latest assessment pattern. A self-assessment at the beginning of Coursebooks 2–8 acts as a useful diagnostic tool.

Language Companions 1–8 comprise extensive reading comprehension, composition, and integrated grammar and vocabulary tasks. It is designed for practice and reinforcement of the concepts taught in the Coursebooks. All topics are mapped to the respective Coursebooks and can be used for independent practice. The Language Companions for classes 3 to 8 also include SAFAL (Structured Assessments for Analyzing Learning) assessments.

Supplementary Readers 1–8 have been designed in keeping with the NCF's focus on 'drop everything and read'. The simple yet high-quality reading material has been curated to inculcate the habit of reading in learners. These books will introduce them to a wide variety of literary genres by both Indian and global authors.

Teacher's Resource Books 1–8 contain lesson plans, additional worksheets, listening transcripts for listening exercises, and answer keys for the Coursebooks, Language Companions, and additional worksheets.

Collins DigiSuite 1–8 comprises multimedia e-books, animations of the reading passages in the Coursebooks, interactivities based on the vocabulary and grammar sections, and a Test Generator for the creation of customized assignments and question papers.

Icons The series prepares learners with the various skills outlined in the NCF 2023. These are tagged with easily recognizable icons.

Twenty-first Century Skills ensure that today's students can thrive in an ever-changing world.

Collaboration, Communication, Creativity, Critical Thinking, Initiative, Leadership, Media Literacy, Productivity, Flexibility, Information Literacy, Social Skills, Technology Literacy, Innovation

India-Focused content puts the spotlight on the heritage, culture, customs, history and geography of the Indian subcontinent.

Art Integrated Learning is a pedagogic model that integrates the fine arts, performing arts, and photography into teaching.

The **Sustainable Development Goals**, adopted by the United Nations in 2015, are a collection of 17 inter-linked goals designed to achieve a sustainable future for all by 2030.

SUSTAINABLE DEVELOPMENT GOALS

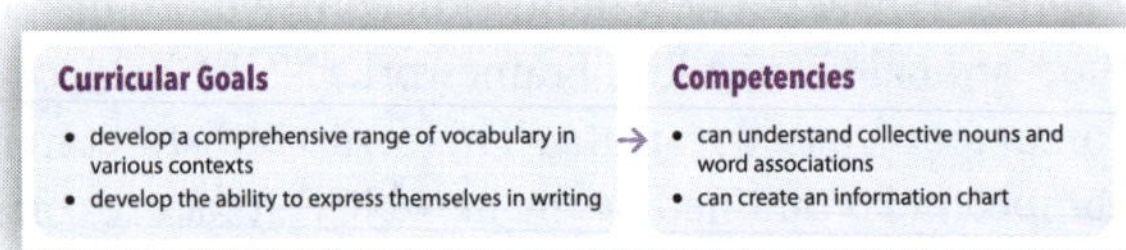

Curricular Goals
- develop a comprehensive range of vocabulary in various contexts
- develop the ability to express themselves in writing

Competencies
- can understand collective nouns and word associations
- can create an information chart

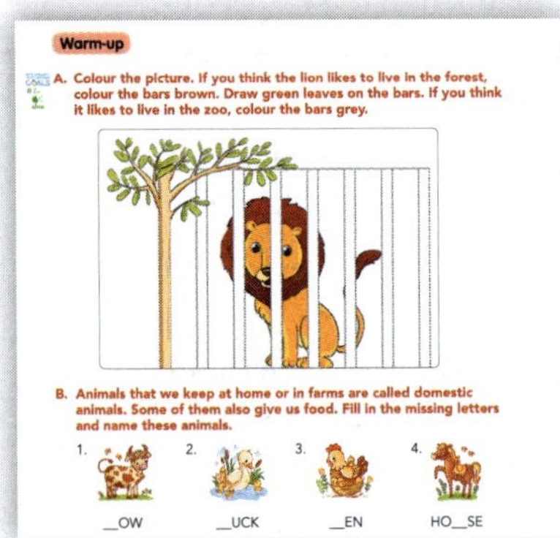

Warm-up

A. Colour the picture. If you think the lion likes to live in the forest, colour the bars brown. Draw green leaves on the bars. If you think it likes to live in the zoo, colour the bars grey.

B. Animals that we keep at home or in farms are called domestic animals. Some of them also give us food. Fill in the missing letters and name these animals.

1. __OW 2. __UCK 3. __EN 4. HO__SE

Warm-up has theme-based activities.

Curricular Goals are mapped to the respective **Competencies** outlined in the NCF 2023.

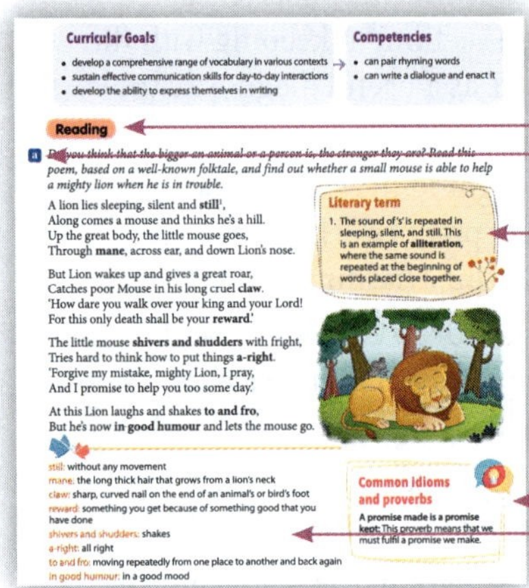

Curricular Goals
- develop a comprehensive range of vocabulary in various contexts
- sustain effective communication skills for day-to-day interactions
- develop the ability to express themselves in writing

Competencies
- can pair rhyming words
- can write a dialogue and enact it

Reading

Do you think that the bigger an animal or a person is, the stronger they are? Read this poem, based on a well-known folktale, and find out whether a small mouse is able to help a mighty lion when he is in trouble.

A lion lies sleeping, silent and **still**[1],
Along comes a mouse and thinks he's a hill.
Up the great body, the little mouse goes,
Through **mane**, across ear, and down Lion's nose.

But Lion wakes up and gives a great roar,
Catches poor Mouse in his long cruel **claw**.
'How dare you walk over your king and your Lord!
For this only death shall be your **reward**.'

The little mouse **shivers and shudders** with fright,
Tries hard to think how to put things **a-right**.
'Forgive my mistake, mighty Lion, I pray,
And I promise to help you too some day.'

At this Lion laughs and shakes **to and fro**,
But he's now **in good humour** and lets the mouse go.

Literary term

1. The sound of 's' is repeated in sleeping, silent, and still. This is an example of **alliteration**, where the same sound is repeated at the beginning of words placed close together.

still: without any movement
mane: the long thick hair that grows from a lion's neck
claw: sharp, curved nail on the end of an animal's or bird's foot
reward: something you get because of something good that you have done
shivers and shudders: shakes
a-right: all right
to and fro: moving repeatedly from one place to another and back again
in good humour: in a good mood

Common idioms and proverbs

A promise made is a promise kept: This proverb means that we must fulfil a promise we make.

Reading comprises a rich variety of texts by global and Indian writers.

All reading passages are accompanied by an animation in **DigiSuite** and tagged by an icon.

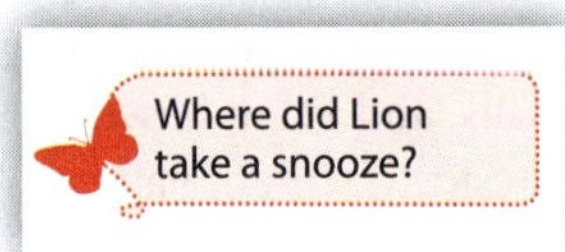

Cross-curricular corner, Literary terms, Common idioms and proverbs have additional trivia, explanations of figures of speech, and idiomatic structures.

While-reading **in-text questions** check factual understanding.

Glossary includes contextual meanings of difficult words.

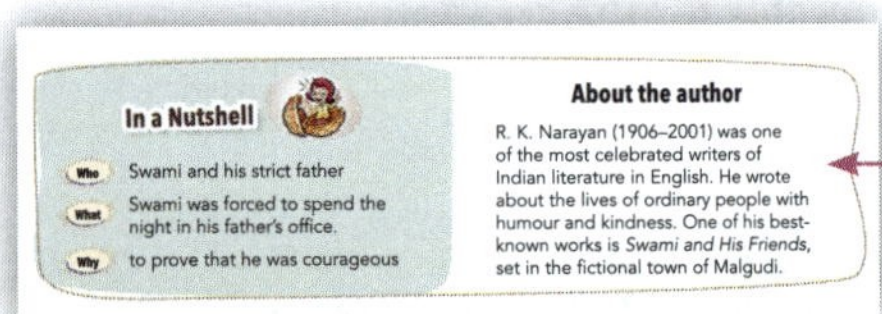

In a Nutshell

Who: Swami and his strict father

What: Swami was forced to spend the night in his father's office.

Why: to prove that he was courageous

About the author

R. K. Narayan (1906–2001) was one of the most celebrated writers of Indian literature in English. He wrote about the lives of ordinary people with humour and kindness. One of his best-known works is *Swami and His Friends*, set in the fictional town of Malgudi.

In a Nutshell is a useful revision tool which recapitulates the key aspects of the text.

About the author/poet/playwright includes a brief biography of the author/poet.

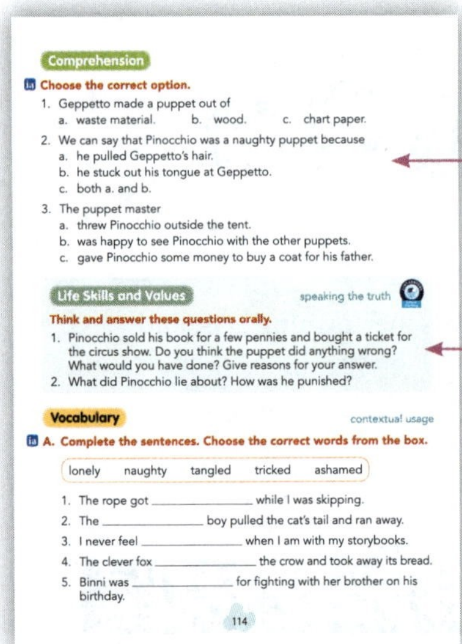

Comprehension

Choose the correct option.

1. Geppetto made a puppet out of
   a. waste material. b. wood. c. chart paper.
2. We can say that Pinocchio was a naughty puppet because
   a. he pulled Geppetto's hair.
   b. he stuck out his tongue at Geppetto.
   c. both a. and b.
3. The puppet master
   a. threw Pinocchio outside the tent.
   b. was happy to see Pinocchio with the other puppets.
   c. gave Pinocchio some money to buy a coat for his father.

Life Skills and Values — speaking the truth

Think and answer these questions orally.

1. Pinocchio sold his book for a few pennies and bought a ticket for the circus show. Do you think the puppet did anything wrong? What would you have done? Give reasons for your answer.
2. What did Pinocchio lie about? How was he punished?

Vocabulary — contextual usage

A. Complete the sentences. Choose the correct words from the box.

lonely naughty tangled tricked ashamed

1. The rope got __________ while I was skipping.
2. The __________ boy pulled the cat's tail and ran away.
3. I never feel __________ when I am with my storybooks.
4. The clever fox __________ the crow and took away its bread.
5. Binni was __________ for fighting with her brother on his birthday.

114

Comprehension checks factual understanding through 'wh-' and objective questions of various types.

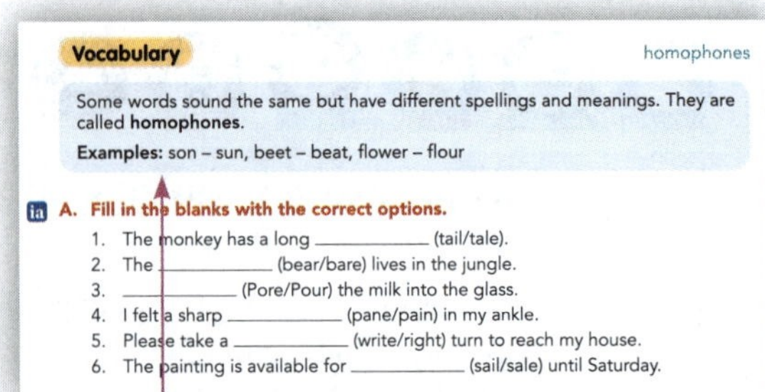

Vocabulary — homophones

Some words sound the same but have different spellings and meanings. They are called **homophones**.

Examples: son – sun, beet – beat, flower – flour

A. Fill in the blanks with the correct options.

1. The monkey has a long __________ (tail/tale).
2. The __________ (bear/bare) lives in the jungle.
3. __________ (Pore/Pour) the milk into the glass.
4. I felt a sharp __________ (pane/pain) in my ankle.
5. Please take a __________ (write/right) turn to reach my house.
6. The painting is available for __________ (sail/sale) until Saturday.

Life Skills and Values has inferential questions on values and interpersonal skills.

Vocabulary includes exercises on contextual usage, modes of language acquisition and figures of speech.

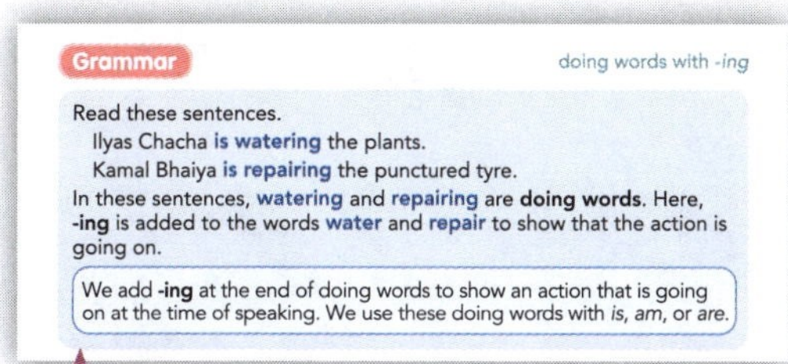
Grammar — doing words with *-ing*

Read these sentences.

Ilyas Chacha **is watering** the plants.

Kamal Bhaiya **is repairing** the punctured tyre.

In these sentences, **watering** and **repairing** are **doing words**. Here, **-ing** is added to the words **water** and **repair** to show that the action is going on.

We add **-ing** at the end of doing words to show an action that is going on at the time of speaking. We use these doing words with *is, am,* or *are.*

Grammar includes graded practice tasks accompanied by simple explanations.

Study Skills includes graded phonics, spelling, and dictionary activities.

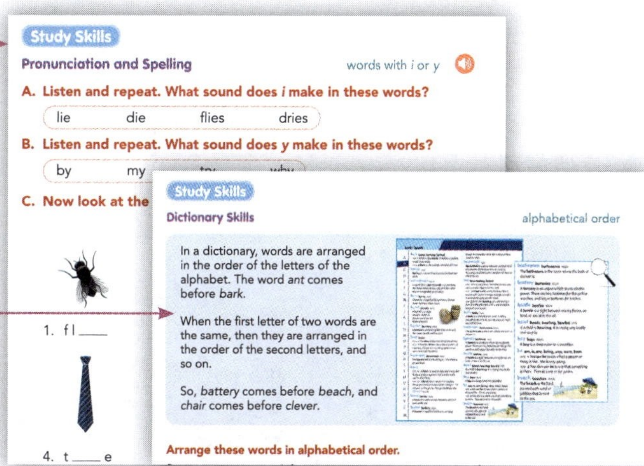
Study Skills

Pronunciation and Spelling — words with *i* or *y*

A. Listen and repeat. What sound does *i* make in these words?

lie die flies dries

B. Listen and repeat. What sound does *y* make in these words?

by my

C. Now look at the

1. fl____

4. t____e

Study Skills

Dictionary Skills — alphabetical order

In a dictionary, words are arranged in the order of the letters of the alphabet. The word *ant* comes before *bark.*

When the first letter of two words are the same, then they are arranged in the order of the second letters, and so on.

So, *battery* comes before *beach,* and *chair* comes before *clever.*

Arrange these words in alphabetical order.

B. How does each member of the family help Bala's mother? Look at the pictures. Match each picture with the person.

Grandpa Father Grandma Bala

Exercises available as interactivities on **DigiSuite** are tagged with an icon.

Listening covers aural comprehension activities, as well as word and sentence-based **Dictation** tasks.

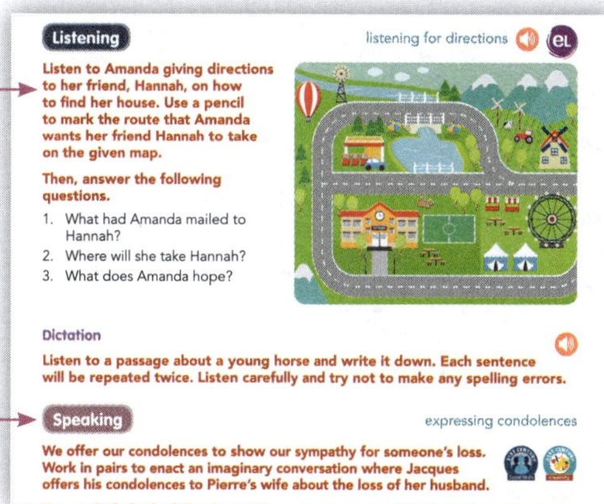
Listening — listening for directions

Listen to Amanda giving directions to her friend, Hannah, on how to find her house. Use a pencil to mark the route that Amanda wants her friend Hannah to take on the given map.

Then, answer the following questions.

1. What had Amanda mailed to Hannah?
2. Where will she take Hannah?
3. What does Amanda hope?

Dictation

Listen to a passage about a young horse and write it down. Each sentence will be repeated twice. Listen carefully and try not to make any spelling errors.

Speaking — expressing condolences

We offer our condolences to show our sympathy for someone's loss. Work in pairs to enact an imaginary conversation where Jacques offers his condolences to Pierre's wife about the loss of her husband.

Speaking includes role plays, conversation practice and public speaking tasks through solo, pair and group work. It also covers financial literacy tasks.

Writing — creating an itinerary

An itinerary is a detailed plan for a journey, including a list of places to visit. Imagine that you and your family will be going away for a vacation during your summer holidays. Work in pairs and plan a day-by-day itinerary for the places you plan to visit.

You can include the following in your itinerary:

- travel options for each day (flight, bus, train)
- details of your arrival and departure
- a rough schedule for various activities, with a short description of each
- local eateries and restaurants that you would visit during your stay

Writing includes graded and free composition. Poetry chapters include **Activity**, a hands-on creative task.

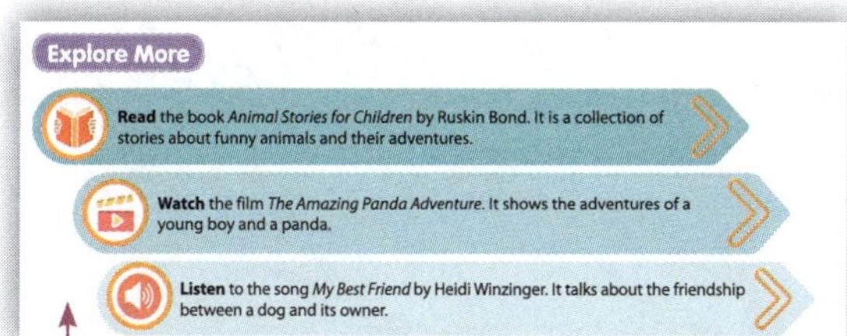
Explore More

Read the book *Animal Stories for Children* by Ruskin Bond. It is a collection of stories about funny animals and their adventures.

Watch the film *The Amazing Panda Adventure*. It shows the adventures of a young boy and a panda.

Listen to the song *My Best Friend* by Heidi Winzinger. It talks about the friendship between a dog and its owner.

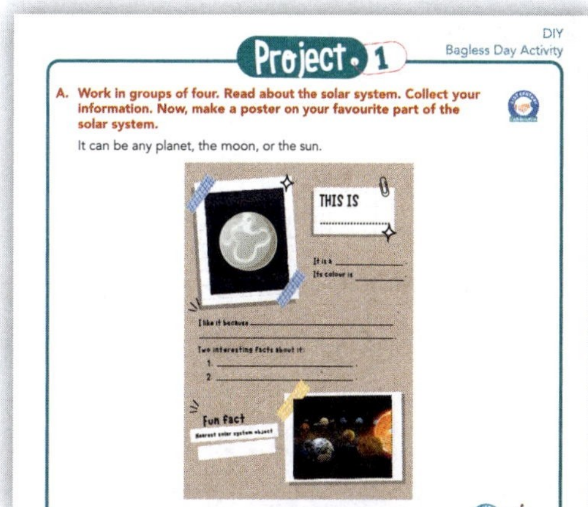
Project 1 — DIY Bagless Day Activity

A. Work in groups of four. Read about the solar system. Collect your information. Now, make a poster on your favourite part of the solar system.

It can be any planet, the moon, or the sun.

Explore More has suggestions for further reading, watching and listening to encourage learners to delve further into the theme of the reading text.

Projects cover cross-curricular activities aligned to the unit themes. They also include 'bagless day' activities.

Detailed Contents

Unit	Chapter	Reading Comprehension	Vocabulary	Grammar	Study Skills	Listening	Speaking	Writing	Activity
Childhood Mischiefs	1. The Special Prize	• MCQ • Questions • Reference to context • Inferential and extrapolative questions	• Contextual usage: crossword • Suffixes	• Parts of speech • Nouns: number and gender	• Spelling: silent letters	• Listening to a passage and making notes	• Interview	• Paragraph writing	
	2. The Incident of the Tooth	• Questions • MCQ • Inferential and extrapolative questions	• Abstract nouns • Idioms	• Nouns: countable and uncountable, singular and plural • Types of pronouns	• Pronunciation: long and short *i*	• Listening to a passage and gap filling • Dictation	• Think-pair-share	• Informal letter	
Quest for Knowledge	3. How I Taught My Grandmother to Read	• Questions • MCQ • Inferential and extrapolative questions	• Words related to books and reading • Forming antonyms with prefixes *dis-*, *un-*, *il-*	• Position of adjectives • Adjectives: degrees of comparison	• Dictionary skills: synonyms	• Listening to a passage and gap filling	• Group discussion	• Message writing	
	4. Children of India	• Tick the correct answer • Questions • Inferential and extrapolative questions	• Commonly confused words • Phrasal verbs	• Subject and predicate • Tenses: simple and continuous	• Spelling: names of professions using *-ian, -ist, -er*	• Listening to a passage and stating true or false	• Participating in a debate	• Formal letter	
Nature and Conservation	5. An Old Friend	• MCQ • Questions • Inferential and extrapolative questions	• Contextual usage	• Punctuation • Agreement of subject and verb	• Spelling: *ie* and *ei* words	• Listening to a passage and stating true or false • Dictation	• Conversation: asking for suggestions	• Writing a story	
	6. *Progress Man*	• MCQ • Questions • Inferential and extrapolative questions	• Compound nouns • Homonyms						• Completing a fact sheet
Project 1	• Class visit to another school		• Designing a brochure						
Fantasy	7. Turkish Delight	• Questions • Character study • MCQ • Inferential and extrapolative questions	• Contextual usage: crossword • Words related to taste	• Direct and indirect speech	• Pronunciation: stressed and unstressed syllables	• Listening to a dialogue and answering questions	• Conversation: making plans	• Picture composition	
	8. *Lord of Tartary*	• MCQ • Questions • Inferential and extrapolative questions	• Rhyming words • Repetition						• Making a poster
Encounters with the Wild	9. An Unexpected Guest	• Completing sentences • Questions • Inferential and extrapolative questions	• Similes	• Transitive and intransitive verbs • Adverbs and their positions	• Dictionary skills: homonyms	• Listening to a poem and gap filling	• Expressing an opinion	• Sequencing and writing a summary	
	10. *A Tiger in the Zoo*	• MCQ • Questions • Inferential and extrapolative questions	• Imagery • Onomatopoeia						• Making a presentation

Community and Neighbourhood	11. A Spark Neglected Burns the House	• Questions • MCQ • Inferential and extrapolative questions	• Synonyms • Proverbs	• Articles • Conjunctions to express reason	• Spelling: words with *-ary*, *-ery* and *-ory*	• Listening to a news report and completing sentences	• Role play: expressing emotions	• Describing people	
	12. *The Palki Song*	• Mind map • Questions • Fill in the blanks, true and false, MCQ • Inferential and extrapolative questions	• *-ing* adjectives • Alliteration						• Writing short descriptions
Project 2	• 'Connect-with-Our-Elders Week'		• Creating a scrapbook						
Food and Celebrations	13. The Theft of the Ruby	• Sequencing • MCQ • Inferential and extrapolative questions	• Words related to celebrations • Verbs with similar meaning	• Tenses: perfect and perfect continuous • Describing past using *would* and *used to*	• Dictionary skills: words of French origin	• Listening to a passage and stating true or false • Dictation	• Enacting the story as a play	• Writing a notice	
	14. *I Wave Good-bye When Butter Flies*	• MCQ • Reference to context • Inferential and extrapolative questions	• Homophones • Pun						• Creating an advertisement
History	15. The Christmas Truce	• MCQ • Questions • Inferential and extrapolative questions	• Contextual usage • Idioms related to the army	• Types of sentences • Prepositions of place and time	• Pronunciation: words with silent consonants	• Listening to a passage and gap filling	• Narrating a chain story	• Diary entry	
	16. *This Morning is Our History Test*	• MCQ • Questions • Inferential and extrapolative questions	• Rhyming couplets						• Data interpretation
Overcoming Odds	17. Journey to a Lost Royal Lair	• Sequencing • MCQ • Questions • Inferential and extrapolative questions	• Collocations • One-word substitutes	• Apostrophe to show possession	• Spelling: words with *au* sound	• Listening to a passage and answering questions	• Giving a speech	• Writing an article for the school magazine	
	18. *A Psalm of Life*	• MCQ • Questions • Inferential and extrapolative questions	• Metaphor						• Writing a poem
Project 3	• Food traditions related to celebrations			• Class discussion and making a presentation					

Self-Assessment

Complete the test to find out how much you already know.

A. Tick [✓] the correct sentence in each pair. (5 × 1)

1. Everyone in the class are making noise. ▢
   Everyone in the class is making noise. ▢
2. The singer and a few other musicians is organizing a special concert. ▢
   The singer and a few other musicians are organizing a special concert. ▢
3. Each of the dancers moves beautifully. ▢
   Each of the dancers move beautifully. ▢
4. Either Kabir or Faizan are going to help with the party. ▢
   Either Kabir or Faizan is going to help with the party. ▢
5. A bouquet of yellow roses was given to the judge. ▢
   A bouquet of yellow roses were given to the judge. ▢

B. Rearrange the given words to make meaningful sentences.
Add the correct punctuation mark at the end of each sentence. (5 × 1)

1. comfort / loud / the / for / too / my / music / is

   ____

2. poet / the / trying / this poem / what / to say / through / is

   ____

3. cross / the street / signal / green / when / do not / is / the

   ____

4. the / melodious / pitter-patter / raindrops / is / the / of / how / falling

   ____

5. the / close / please / the doors / all / windows / going out / and / before

   ____

C. Complete the passage with the correct prepositions. You may have to use some prepositions more than once. (10 × 0.5)

to in at of for on

I stood __________ the field, shocked. Now, because __________ my foolish behaviour, the whole team was going to suffer. A team member should always work __________ the betterment __________ the team. But what had I done? I went back __________ my desk and sat quietly __________ my chair. After thinking __________ a while, I knew what I should do. I took a sheet of paper and wrote my apology letter __________ it. I went __________ my coach's chamber and gave him the letter. Then I stood __________ the door waiting for him to read it.

D. Match Column A with Column B to make meaningful sentences and circle the conjunctions. (5 × 1)

Column A	Column B
1. The crow flew low	a. because it's not healthy.
2. We can go to the science exhibition	b. but it did not run away.
3. We should avoid fast food	c. and dived into the water.
4. The cat was startled	d. so we moved to a safer place.
5. It wasn't safe to remain at the accident spot,	e. or attend the debate.

E. Write the opposites of the given words. (5 × 1)

1. rare __________
2. create __________
3. disagree __________
4. major __________
5. punish __________

F. Look at the picture clues and write the correct homophones for each sentence. (5 × 1)

1. I have been feeling __________ for a __________.

2. I would like two __________ of __________, please.

3. The fighting countries made __________ after a __________ of territory was handed over.

4. The __________ arrived at the castle last __________.

5. Some tribes __________ before hunting their __________.

The answers are given on page 42.

Assessment

1. If you score 3 or more in each section, you are ready to start English Expert Coursebook 6.
2. If you score less than 3 in section A, revise 'agreement of subject and verb'.
3. If you score less than 3 in section B, revise 'sentences'.
4. If you score less than 3 in section C, revise 'prepositions'.
5. If you score less than 3 in section D, revise 'conjunctions'.
6. If you score less than 3 in section E, revise 'opposites'.
7. If you score less than 3 in section F, revise 'homophones'.

UNIT I

Childhood Mischiefs

Warm-up

A. We can sometimes develop a mistaken understanding of people around us based on the way they appear. Think of a time when you thought a person appeared to be rude and unkind. But later, you found that they were nice and polite. Use the given mind map to describe why you viewed the person the way you did.

first impression of the person

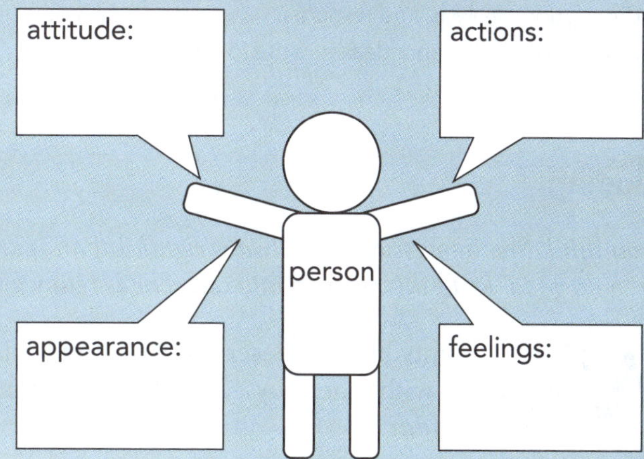

B. Match these literary characters, who are known to make up tall stories and tell lies, with their descriptions.

21ST CENTURY Information Literacy

Character	Description
1. Voldemort	a. This naughty wooden puppet is a liar by habit. Every time he lies, his nose grows longer.
2. Alice	b. This bored young girl dreams of a world of talking animals and other fantastical creatures.
3. Pinocchio	c. He loves having sugar but repeatedly denies having it when asked by his father.
4. Sheriff of Nottingham	d. This leader of dark wizards will stop at no lie or misdeed to get what he wants: the young wizard who caused him to lose all his powers.
5. Johnny	e. This greedy man always looks for opportunities to take money from the poor. However, he is outsmarted by Robin Hood's band of outlaws.

short story

1

The Special Prize

Anant Dev Sharma

Curricular Goals

- develop a comprehensive range of vocabulary in various contexts
- identify the basic linguistic aspects such as parts of speech and use them in oral and written expression
- effective communication using language skills for description, analysis, and response
- organize thoughts and ideas to write for an intended purpose

Competencies

- can use contextual words and suffixes
- can identify the parts of speech and apply the concepts of gender and number in nouns
- can identify silent letters in words
- can conduct an interview and write a paragraph on a given topic

Reading

a *Do you think first impressions are always right? Tapan is known to everyone as the boy who is up to no good. Read this story to find out if he is really a troublemaker.*

INDIA FOCUS

'What a naughty boy! He deserves to be thrashed. I have also received reports of his getting into fights with other boys. Send for him. Mohan! Hey, Mohan!' the headmaster shouted for the ***chowkidar***.

Mohan rushed in and asked nervously, 'Yes, sir?'

'Hurry, and get Tapan of Class V,' the headmaster ordered.

Tapan was the second son of Ratan, the clerk of Padumani village.

Although rather thin, he was strong, somewhat dark and had bright eyes.

He was quite good at his studies, but he was always getting into trouble.

He was never the first to pick a quarrel. But if anybody upset him, he didn't stop to give as good as he got[1].

Common idioms and phrases

1. **give as good as you get:** This idiom means to argue, fight or compete as fiercely as your opponent.

He had only been at Jnanpeeth a month and already there was a complaint against him. Haren, the shopkeeper of Padumani village, had complained to the headmaster that Tapan and a few other boys had thrown stones at his shop the previous evening.

Tapan came in and after glancing **timidly** at the headmaster, stood with his head lowered.

What was the name of Tapan's father?

'You are Tapan, aren't you?'

'Do you know this gentleman?' the headmaster asked, pointing at the shopkeeper.

'Yes, sir. He lives in our village.'

'Well, is it true that last evening you and your friends threw stones at his shop?'

chowkidar: a gatekeeper or a watchman

timidly: shy and nervously

'Yes, sir.'

'Why? Why did you do that? Answer me!' the headmaster thundered.

'Sir, this man charges higher prices and cheats by way of weight too. The day before yesterday, we bought a kilogram of dal from him. When we weighed it at home, it turned out to be only 800 grams. When I asked him about it, he chased me out of his shop. That is why we threw stones at his shop.'

The headmaster looked at the shopkeeper, whose face was red.

He thought for some time. Then turning to Tapan, he said, 'Even so, what you did was not right. If the shopkeeper is dishonest, it is for the village panchayat to take up the matter. Hold out your hand!' Tapan received five strokes of the cane. When he returned to his class, his classmates laughed and made fun of him.

A few days later, a fierce ox began disturbing the locality. If anyone approached it with a stick, it would charge at them.

The rudeness of the animal awoke Tapan's spirit. 'Wait, you big bully! I will tame you,' he mumbled.

During lunch break, he approached the ox slowly with a stick and a piece of string. He jumped onto its back and put the rope across its mouth. The ox was taken by surprise, but the moment it felt the boy's weight on its back, it broke into a gallop hoping to throw him off.

Meanwhile, the break was over, and classes had started, but Tapan was busy taming the ox. He had managed to keep himself on the back of the tossing, leaping beast by holding the string firmly. He patted the ox's back.

That further angered the animal. It crashed into the school compound and then into the seventh standard classroom. The teacher and the students screamed and scattered in all directions. Many of them stumbled and fell.

Several glass panes were shattered by the horns of the wildly **prancing** animal. Then, the tired and confused creature ran mooing desperately into the school field and fell on its side. A few seconds later it jumped up and ran for its life, without a backward glance.

What did the ox do when Tapan tried to tame it?

prancing: moving quickly with high steps

So, another complaint was lodged against Tapan, this time by the class teacher – Rajani Saharia – though he had managed to escape unhurt. The headmaster flew into a rage[2]. Not only the students but the school building had also suffered.

He called Tapan again.

'You are a wicked boy! Why did you lead the ox into the classroom? Speak up!' the headmaster.

> **Common idioms and phrases**
>
> 2. **fly into a rage:** This idiom means to get very angry suddenly.

Tapan replied, head lowered, 'Sir, I didn't lead the ox into the classroom. I was only riding on its back to tame it, and it suddenly ran into the room.'

'Who asked you to ride an ox during school hours? Go and stand outside the classroom.'

Tapan's classmates heard of his latest misadventure and again made fun of him. He was called the 'bad boy' of the school. A few boys came out of their classes pretending to do something else and made faces at him.

The same day, the headmaster was taking his usual evening walk. Dusk was falling when he saw Tapan. He was holding an old beggar woman's hand. On his head, he carried her begging basket. Two boys of his class walked alongside them, laughing and making rude remarks: Naren, the one who had topped in his class, and his friend, Mahesh.

The old woman had a fever. She could hardly walk, leave alone carry her basket. Seeing her condition, Tapan had lifted her basket on his head and taking the old woman's hand had said, 'Granny, hold on to me. I'll walk you home.'

When Naren and Mahesh saw the headmaster, they greeted him and looked at Tapan with a smile, pleased that he was seeing one of Tapan's misdeeds himself.

When the headmaster questioned the old woman, she replied, voice trembling, 'Had this dear boy not been there, I would still have been lying on the road. May God shower him with blessings! The two boys there also saw how ill I was but they didn't help me.

Why did Naren and Mahesh look at Tapan with a smile?

The headmaster scolded Naren and Mahesh and sent them away. He asked Tapan to take the old woman home.

Two weeks later, the headmaster was again returning from his walk. He saw an ox lying on the ground. Its leg was broken. Kneeling beside it was Tapan, applying medicine and bandaging its leg. There were tears in his eyes. He was startled when the headmaster came and stood near him.

The headmaster asked, 'What are you doing here, Tapan?'

'Sir, some wicked boys have broken the ox's leg. It is in great pain. Is it not wrong to hurt animals?'

'Didn't you ride this same ox the other day, saying that it was wicked and needed to be tamed? How has it become so good in your eyes today?'

Cross-curricular Corner

Dr B. R. Ambedkar was a lawyer, social reformer and political leader who headed the committee which wrote the Indian constitution.

'Well, sir, it was very wicked. But it has changed its ways. It has not only stopped attacking people but also makes way for them. I have chewed a few medicinal leaves and dressed the injured leg with the **pulp**. They are very good for injuries, sir,' Tapan said.

The headmaster stood deep in thought. Then he looked at the boy's face and affectionately patted him. Without a word, he started on his way home. His eyes were moist.

Common idioms and phrases

3. **the ground would swallow you up:** This idiom refers to the feeling of wanting to disappear because of something that might cause shame.

A few weeks later was the prize-giving day of Jnanpeeth High School. This time the headmaster had decided to award a special prize to the student with the best character. Three books – the biographies of Mahatma Gandhi, Jawaharlal Nehru, and Dr B. R. Ambedkar – were to be given away as the prize. In Tapan's classroom, Naren said loudly to Bhabesh, 'Do you know that the special prize for the best character is being awarded to Tapan?'

The boys roared with laughter. Tapan's face grew red. He wished the ground would swallow him up[3].

The function started. After the usual speeches came the distribution of prizes. Addressing the assembly, the headmaster announced, 'Honourable guests, we have decided to give the special prize for the student with the best character to Shriman Tapan Hazarika of Class V.'

The teachers and students were astonished. The faces of Naren and Bhabesh were a sight to see.

Tapan could not believe his ears.

The headmaster repeated, 'Tapan Kumar Hazarika, Class V.'

Why did the headmaster affectionately pat Tapan?

pulp: soft, wet paste made by crushing something

Could it be true that Tapan, known as the 'bad boy' of the school, was being called to receive the prize? He stood up and went up to the stage.

The headmaster then narrated how Tapan had helped the old beggar woman and nursed the injured ox. He also gave Tapan five rupees from his own pocket. The hall echoed with applause.

Tapan's heart almost burst with joy and pride.

In a Nutshell

Who Tapan, a young boy, and the headmaster of his school

What Tapan received a special prize for his kindness.

Where at his school

Why He helped an old lady and an injured ox.

Comprehension

HOTS

ia **A. Answer the questions.**

1. Why did the shopkeeper's face turn red when Tapan explained to the headmaster why he had thrown stones? Choose the correct option.
   a. The shopkeeper was angry. ☐
   b. The shopkeeper was shy. ☐
   c. The shopkeeper was ashamed. ☐
2. Naren and Mahesh thought that the headmaster would scold Tapan for talking to and helping the beggar woman.
   State 'true' or 'false'. Correct the statement if it is false. ______________________
3. How did Tapan help the injured ox? Tick [✓] all the correct options.
   a. He chewed medicinal leaves to make pulp. ☐
   b. He bandaged the injured leg after applying the medicine. ☐
   c. He helped the ox get up and took it home. ☐
4. Circle the words that you think describe Tapan.

strong	obedient	sensitive	cruel
studious	kind	brave	helpful

5. *Tapan's face grew red. He wished the ground would swallow him up.*
   a. Why did Tapan's face grow red?
   b. Explain the meaning of 'He wished the ground would swallow him up'.
6. What lesson do you learn from the story? Choose the correct option.
   a. We should obey our elders and focus on studying. ☐
   b. We should help others and be kind to them. ☐

B. Answer the questions in a few lines.

1. How did the shopkeeper cheat his customers? What impression do you form of him?
2. 'If the shopkeeper is dishonest, it is for the village panchayat to take up the matter.' Do you agree with the speaker? Why/Why not?
3. What impression of Tapan do you have at the beginning of the story?
4. Why were the headmaster's eyes moist when he left Tapan with the injured ox?
5. Tapan got punished for two 'misdeeds' and was rewarded for the other two. How do you think the incidents were different? Do you think he was rightly punished for the first two actions?

Life Skills and Values

intentions and actions, humour

1. Do you think the headmaster was right to hit Tapan for throwing stones at the shop?
2. Did you find any incident in the story funny? Give examples.

Vocabulary

contextual usage: crossword

A. Complete the crossword with words from the story, using the clues.

Across

2. an unlucky event
4. the noise made by a group of people clapping their hands in appreciation
5. morally bad
6. in a way that shows no confidence in oneself

Down

1. an angry argument
3. spoke very loudly or angrily

suffixes

Look at these words.

desperate**ly** honour**able**

These words are formed by adding suffixes to the words *desperate* and *honour*.

Suffixes are groups of letters added after a word to form a new word. The new word can be an adjective, an adverb or a noun.

B. Match the words with the suffixes to make new words. Then, fill in the blanks with the words you have made.

colour	comfort	magic
bright	free	entertain

-ness	-ment	-ful
-al	-dom	-able

1. The king was believed to have __________ powers, with which he could control dragons.
2. Ria tried her best to make the guests feel __________.
3. The children love the __________ walls of the classroom, painted by the teachers themselves.
4. The __________ of the summer sun blurred my vision for a moment.
5. __________ fighters like Bhagat Singh and Khudiram Bose sacrificed their lives for the country.
6. The radio is the old man's only source of __________.

Grammar

parts of speech

We use different words to convey the meaning of a sentence. There are eight parts of speech in the English language – noun, pronoun, verb, adjective, adverb, preposition, conjunction and interjection.

Example: Aargh! Tapan quickly jumped onto the angry bull's back and tamed it.

Aargh! → interjection; Tapan → noun; quickly → adverb; jumped → verb; onto → preposition; the → article; angry → adjective; and → conjunction; tamed → verb; it → pronoun

A. Identify the parts of speech in the paragraph and complete the table.

The same day, the headmaster was taking his usual evening walk. Dusk was falling. He saw Tapan. He was holding an old beggar woman's hand. On his head, he carried her begging basket. Two boys of his class walked alongside them: Naren and his friend, Mahesh.

Noun	Pronoun	Verb	Adverb	Adjective	Preposition	Conjunction

nouns: number and gender

You know that a noun is **singular** when it refers to one person or thing and **plural** when it refers to more than one person or thing.

Examples: Tapan was called the bad **boy** of the school.

Sir, some wicked **boys** have broken the ox's leg.

You also know that nouns tell us whether a person or animal is of masculine or feminine gender.

Example: The old **lady** blessed the **boy** for his kindness. (*lady*: feminine, *boy*: masculine)

Nouns are of **common gender** if they are the same whether they refer to the masculine or the feminine gender. Nouns are of **neuter gender** if they refer to non-living things or groups of living things.

Example: The **shopkeeper** chased me out of his **shop**. (*shopkeeper*: common, *shop*: neuter)

ia **B. Fill in the blanks with the plural forms of the nouns in brackets. Then, state their gender.**

1. The old ____________ (vixen) trotted through the ____________ (neighbourhood) looking for scraps of food.
2. The ____________ (drake) dove into the water at the first sign of danger.
3. The ____________ (groom) refused to ride ____________ (horse).
4. Moira planted ____________ (peony) in the small garden behind her house.
5. The ____________ (ox) refused to pull the ____________ (plough) under the hot, summer sun.
6. Koireng's ____________ (sister-in-law) set up a clothing business last year.

Study Skills

Spelling

silent letters

A **silent letter** is a letter that is used to spell a word, but its sound is not pronounced while saying the word.

Examples: Do you **k**now that the special prize is being awarded to Tapan?
Is it not **w**rong to hurt animals?

Underline the words with silent letters in the passage.

The poor orphan boy sat on a ledge on the edge of the river. A yacht passed under a bridge and the boy dreamt of foreign lands. Here, in autumn, rhinos guarded castles in which knights lived. The boy bit his thumb and said, 'I know! I could write a tale, filled with lovely adjectives, and build my own world.'

Listening

listening for details

Listen to a passage about a hardworking gentleman and complete the notes.

1. The narrator's father came to this place: ____________________
2. He came from this country: ____________________
3. He taught himself this: ____________________

4. At night, he worked here: ______________________

5. At the eatery, he had these responsibilities ______________________

6. He worked as a clerk here: ______________________

7. He wrote these at first: ______________________

8. He retired at this age: ______________________

Speaking

interview

Imagine that you are a student journalist at Tapan's school. After his surprise win, you decide to interview him for the school's newspaper. In pairs, enact an interview, with one of you as the interviewer and the other as Tapan.

You can begin the interview with the following dialogue:

Interviewer: Congratulations, Tapan! How are you feeling?

Tapan: Thank you! I am surprised and very happy.

Interviewer: Did you expect to win?

Tapan: Not at all! I thought that the headmaster was upset with me.

Interviewer: Can you guess why he chose you?

Writing

paragraph writing

Do you think punishment is necessary to maintain discipline? Write a paragraph on the topic. You can consider the following points:

- Can discipline be maintained in any other way, such as through open communication?
- Is punishment the only way to keep order in large classrooms?
- If you were a teacher, what would you do to ensure discipline in your classroom?

Explore More

Read the book *George's Marvellous Medicine* by Roald Dahl, about the misadventures of George, as he tries to make a medicine for his grandmother.

Watch the 1990 film *Home Alone* by Chris Columbus. It is about an eight-year-old troublemaker and his adventures as he defends his house from burglars.

graphic story

2 The Incident of the Tooth

Mark Twain

Curricular Goals

- identify literary devices and idioms by reading a variety of literature
- recognize basic linguistic aspects and use them in oral and written expression
- express through speech ideas on various aspects of social and cultural surroundings
- write different kinds of letters in appropriate style and register for different audiences and purposes

Competencies

- can understand the meaning and usage of idioms
- can correctly use different types of nouns and pronouns
- can pronounce words with long *i* and short *i* sounds
- can narrate an anecdote and write an informal letter

Reading

a *Have you ever made up a story so that you could skip school and stay home? This story is based on an extract from the book,* The Adventures of Tom Sawyer, *set in the fictional town of St Petersberg in nineteenth century America. Tom is an orphan who lives with his Aunt Polly, his half-brother, Sid and his cousin Mary. Read on to find out what happens when Tom comes up with imaginative tales to avoid school.*

Why did Tom not like Monday mornings?

But the **colicky** symptoms soon grew **feeble**, and soon, died wholly away. He **reflected** further, and discovered that one of his upper front teeth was loose.

Tom decided to **hold** the tooth **in reserve** for the present and seek further.

Then he remembered hearing the doctor speaking about a certain illness that laid up a patient for two or three weeks. One could even lose a finger from it.

Tom began groaning with spirit, but Sid slept on unconscious.

Tom groaned louder and **fancied** that he began to feel pain in the toe.

There was no response from Sid.

Tom was panting with his **exertions** by this time. He rested a moment and then swelled himself up and fetched a **succession** of admirable groans.

Sid snored on.

colicky: associated with a stomach ache
feeble: weak
reflected: thought
hold in reserve: keep something available for later use
sore: painful and often, red
fancied: imagined
exertions: great efforts that make someone tired
succession: (here) series

joggle, stir: shake

handsomely: (here) successfully
window sash: window frame
rubbage: (here) rubbish

mortified: affected by gangrene, a serious condition which causes tissues in the body to decay

restored: brought back to normal condition

turn: a short period of feeling quite unwell

ceased: stopped

Cross-curricular Corner

A common home remedy for removing a loose tooth was to tie a string to it and push a glowing coal towards the person's face. Fear of the burning coal would make their head jerk away. Meanwhile, the string, whose other end was tied to a stationary object, would pull the tooth in the opposite direction, thus getting it out.

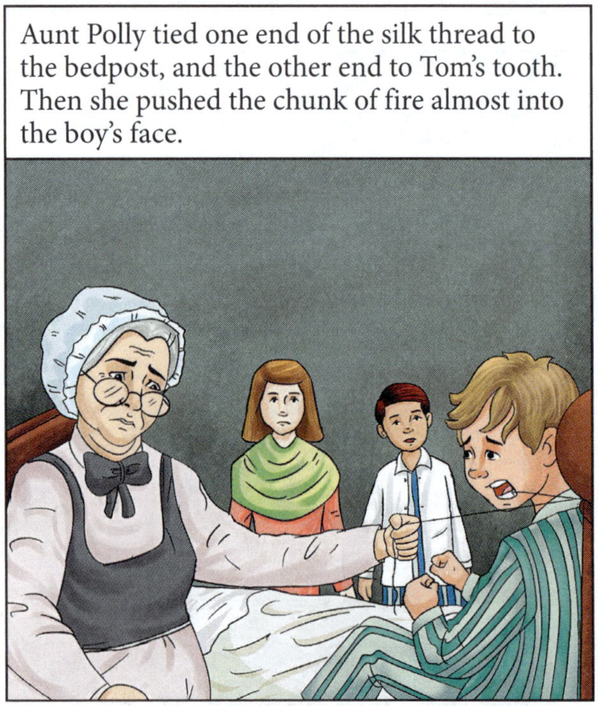

Why did Tom lie to everyone?

row: (here) trouble, noise

outrageousness: shocking acts that cross the limits of reason

Common idioms and proverbs

play truant: This idiom means to stay away from school without permission or a genuine reason.

The tooth hung dangling by the bedpost.

But difficult times also bring their rewards. When Tom went to school later that day, he was the envy of every boy because the gap in his upper row of teeth allowed him to spit in a new way. He gathered quite a following of lads interested in the **exhibition**.

exhibition: show

In a Nutshell

- **Who** Tom, Sid, Aunt Polly, Mary
- **What** Tom's loose tooth is pulled out.
- **How** with the help of a thread and a chunk of fire
- **Why** The tooth was loose. But, Tom didn't want to use this as his excuse for missing school.
- **Where** at home in Aunt Polly's house

About the author

Mark Twain (1835–1910), whose real name was Samuel Langhorne Clemens, was an American author best known for his books, *The Adventures of Tom Sawyer* and *The Adventures of Huckleberry Finn*. Twain based the books on his childhood memories and experiences.

Comprehension

A. Answer the questions.

1. Why did Tom dislike attending school on Mondays?
2. Why did Tom decide to hold the tooth in reserve? What did he think of next?
3. Why did Tom get annoyed with Sid?
4. What did Aunt Polly ask Mary to fetch?
5. According to Aunt Polly, what did Tom do to break her heart?
6. 'But difficult times also bring their rewards.' What was Tom's reward?
7. Do you think Aunt Polly was a sensible woman? Give reasons for your answer.

ia HOTS

B. Tick [✓] the correct answers.

1. *'Oh, auntie, my sore toe's mortified!' The old lady sank into the chair.*
   Why do you think the old lady sank into the chair?
   a. She was frail. b. She was relieved. c. She was shocked.
2. Tom's groans stopped because ________________.
   a. he was tired b. his tooth was removed c. his lie was found out
3. Which of the following did Aunt Polly not use to pull out Tom's tooth?
   a. the bedpost b. a silk thread c. a knife
4. Tom's tooth was taken out ________________.
   a. sadly b. forcibly c. carefully
5. When Sid woke up, he shook Tom and looked at his face ________________.
   a. anxiously b. happily c. doubtfully
6. *Tom <u>fancied</u> that he began to feel pain in the toe.*
   Which word is a suitable replacement for the underlined word?
   a. imagined b. liked c. wanted

Life Skills and Values

being responsible, honesty

21ST CENTURY Social Skills · 21ST CENTURY Critical Thinking

1. Do you think it is important to consider how our actions can affect others? Explain with examples from the story.
2. Can lies be dangerous? Give reasons for your answer.
3. Did you think the story was funny? Which sections made you laugh? Explain in your own words.

Vocabulary

abstract nouns

Abstract nouns refer to things which we cannot see or touch but only feel. They include feelings, experiences, states, qualities and ideas.

Example: Tom was suffering in reality now, so handsomely was his **imagination** working.

Abstract nouns can be formed from verbs or adjectives.

Examples: behave → **behaviour** speak → **speech** happy → **happiness**

They are often formed by adding a suffix to the verb or adjective. Sometimes, the word may need to be changed before the suffix is added.

Examples: silly → **silliness** communicate → **communication**

ia A. Form abstract nouns from these words from the story and use them to fill in the blanks.

ill think difficult discovered admirable annoyed

1. The scientist's work led to an important ____________.
2. I have the greatest ____________ for those who help animals.
3. The doctor prescribed three types of medicines for her ____________.
4. I share all my ____________, both happy and sad, with my best friend.
5. The loudspeakers are causing ____________ to everyone in the area.
6. We found the house without any ____________ because of the host's clear directions.

idioms

An **idiom** is a group of words whose meaning is different from the meanings of the individual words. It is usually a combination of a noun and a verb.

Examples: It **makes my flesh crawl** to hear you. (to feel afraid or horrified by something)

Tom, what **a turn** you did **give** me. (frighten or shock somebody)

ia B. Match the idioms with their meanings.

Idiom	Meaning
1. spill the beans	a. change one's way of life to become a better, more responsible person
2. turn over a new leaf	b. not share the same views as somebody about something
3. cost an arm and a leg	c. receiving the benefits of two completely different situations at the same time
4. the best of both worlds	d. very expensive
5. not see eye to eye	e. tell a secret

Now, make sentences of your own with any three idioms.

Grammar

nouns: countable and uncountable, singular and plural

Read this sentence.
Mary, get me some silk **threads**, and a chunk of **fire** out of the kitchen.

Here, the noun *threads* is **countable**. You know that countable nouns can be singular or plural. The word *fire* is an **uncountable noun**.

Language Booster

Not all nouns that end with *s* are plural countable nouns.

Examples: *measles, mathematics, billiards*

ia **A. Read these lines from the story and identify the underlined nouns as countable (C) or uncountable (UC).**

But difficult times also bring their rewards. When Tom went to school later that day, he was the envy of every boy because the gap in his upper row of teeth allowed him to spit in a new way. He felt joy as they gathered around to watch him show off his new skill.

types of pronouns

You know that pronouns are words that are used in place of nouns to avoid repetition. They are of several types.

Personal pronouns are used in place of the names of people and things. These are *I, we, you, he, she, it, they, me, us, him, her* and *them.*

Examples: **It** occurred to **him** that **he** wished he were sick.

Possessive pronouns are used to show ownership and belonging. They are *mine, yours, his, hers, ours, its* and *theirs.*

Example: The one-eyed cat is **his**.

Reflexive pronouns are used when we want to refer back to the subject of the sentence. They are *myself, yourself, himself, herself, oneself, itself, ourselves, yourselves,* and *themselves.*

Example: He swelled **himself** up and fetched a succession of admirable groans.

ia **B. Fill in the blanks with the given pronouns.**

herself itself mine she theirs ourselves it hers

1. The books in the cupboard are __________ alone. But the books with Nafisa's name on them are __________.
2. Sally bought a bouquet of flowers for __________.
3. Riya sings so beautifully. __________ takes lessons from a famous musician.
4. Mr and Mrs Apte have known Jacob for years. He is an old neighbour of __________ from Nashik.
5. The cat hissed angrily. Then, __________ began swishing its tail from side to side.
6. The dog looked at __________ in the mirror and barked.
7. We found __________ alone on the empty road, with not a soul in sight.

Study Skills

Pronunciation

long and short *i* sounds

Look at these word pairs and say them aloud. The first word in each pair has the short *i* sound, while the second word has the long *i* sound.

bit – bite **pin – pine** **fit – fine**

Read the words aloud and write them in the correct columns.

pipe time sit flight like shin din dine pick shine

short *i* sound as in *pin*	long *i* sound as in *pine*

Listening

listening for facts

Listen to a passage about Mark Twain and fill in the blanks.

1. Mark Twain got his sense of humour from his ______________.
2. Twain had ______________ siblings.
3. His mother's name was ______________.
4. Twain suffered from ______________ till he was ten years old.
5. He would test his mother's patience through ______________.
6. Years later, when Twain asked his mother if she had been worried that he would not live, she responded, 'I was ______________ you would.'

Dictation

You will now listen to a short passage about Tom Sawyer. Write it down. Each sentence will be repeated twice. Listen carefully and try to not make any spelling errors.

Speaking

think-pair-share (financial literacy)

21ST CENTURY Collaboration 21ST CENTURY Communication

Imagine that Tom was genuinely unwell and had to be taken to the hospital. How do you think people made payments in hospitals in the nineteenth century? Do you think they had cheque books, or did they have to make cash payments? How have modes of payment changed since then? In groups of four, discuss the topic. Then, take turns, in groups, to share your point of view with the class.

Writing

informal letter

Creativity

In the story, Tom realises that sometimes our mischiefs may come back to bite us. Imagine that you are Tom. Write a humorous letter to your best friend, Huckleberry Finn, telling him about the incident and the lesson you have learnt.

You may include the following points:

- why you came up with the plan
- the various illnesses you thought of
- how you were outsmarted
- your feeling of embarrassment when caught out

Explore More

Read the book *Adventures of Huckleberry Finn* by Mark Twain. It is about the exciting twists and turns in the life of Tom Sawyer's rebellious friend, Huckleberry Finn.

Watch the 1993 film *Dennis the Menace* by Nick Castle about the mischiefs of five-year-old Dennis Mitchell when he is left under the care of his neighbours, Mr and Mrs Wilson.

Listen to the song 'The Boy Who Cried Wolf' by the English singer-songwriter, Passenger. It is based on the classic Aesop's fable, 'The Boy Who Cried Wolf', about a boy whom nobody trusts, as he had lied in the past, even when he is telling the truth.

UNIT II

Quest for Knowledge

Warm-up

A. The United Nations Sustainable Development Goal 4 aims to ensure quality education and promote lifelong learning opportunities for all.

Discuss and answer the following questions in class.

1. Why is education necessary?
2. How does literacy, or the ability to read and write, help us gain knowledge?
3. Can someone be knowledgeable without being able to read and write? Can you think of such a person in real life?
4. What are the different ways in which we can educate ourselves and others?

B. Cricket is a very popular game with Indian children. Work in pairs and identify these fielding positions in the game of cricket.

deep   silly point   gully   slip   wicketkeeper   mid-wicket

1. The fielder stands close to the batter and is considered 'silly': __________
2. This player 'keeps' or handles the wicket: __________
3. This fielder stands towards the middle of the wicket: __________
4. This fielder stands close to the wicketkeeper to catch the ball slipping away from the bat: __________
5. This fielder is far away or at the deep end of the field: __________
6. This fielder stands on the narrow strip between point and slip: __________

short story

3

How I Taught My Grandmother to Read

Sudha Murty

Curricular Goals

- comprehend the way words and sentences are used in different subjects across the curriculum
- identify the basic linguistic aspects such as sentence style and parts of speech
- listen carefully and raise probing questions about social experiences
- writes letters, essays and reports in appropriate style and registers for different media, audiences and purposes

Competencies

- can recognize words related to books and reading, and form antonyms using prefixes
- can apply the concept of order of adjectives and understand comparison of adjectives
- can participate in a group discussion and write a message

Reading

a *Imagine how it would feel if you did not know how to read or write. Not every person is fortunate enough to be able to go to school and receive proper education. Read a story about a grandmother who decided to learn to read, without letting her age hold her back.*

INDIA FOCUS

When I was a girl of about twelve, I used to stay in a village in north Karnataka with my grandparents. In those days, the transport system was not very good, so we used to get the morning paper only in the afternoon. All of us would wait eagerly for the bus which used to come with the papers, weekly magazines and the post.

Cross-curricular Corner

A pen name is a name used by a writer instead of their real name. This may be done to hide the author's identity, sometimes by using a short name which inspires them. Triveni is the pen name of the author, Anasuya Shankar. She wrote about issues faced by women.

At that time, Triveni was a very popular writer in the Kannada language. One of her novels, called *Kashi Yatre*, was appearing as a **serial** in the Kannada weekly, *Karmaveera* at the time.

My grandmother, Krishtakka, never went to school. So she could not read. Every Wednesday, *Karmaveera* would come and I would read the next episode of *Kashi Yatre* to her. During that time, she would forget all her work and listen with the greatest concentration. Later, she could repeat the entire text by heart. After hearing what happened next in *Kashi Yatre*, she would join her friends at the temple courtyard where the children would also gather to play hide-and-seek. She would discuss the latest episode with her friends.

Once I went for a wedding with my cousins to the neighbouring village. In those days, a wedding was a great event. We enjoyed ourselves thoroughly. We would eat and play endlessly, **savouring** the freedom because all the elders were busy. I went for a couple of days but ended up staying for a week.

serial: a story on television or the radio, or in a magazine, that is broadcast or published in several separate parts

savouring: enjoying

When I came back to my village, I found my grandmother in tears. I was surprised, for I had never seen her cry even in the most difficult of situations. What had happened? I was worried.

'*Avva*, is everything all right? Are you okay?'

I used to call her *avva*, which means 'mother' in Kannada.

She nodded but did not reply. I did not understand and forgot about it. In the night, after dinner, we were sleeping in the open terrace of the house. It was a summer night and there was a full moon. *Avva* came and sat next to me. Her affectionate hands touched my forehead. I realized she wanted to speak. I asked her, 'What is the matter?'

'When I was a young girl, I lost my mother. There was nobody to look after and guide me. My father was a busy man and got married again. In those days, people never considered education **essential** for girls, so I never went to school. I got married very young and had children. I became very busy. Later, I had grandchildren and always felt so happy cooking and feeding all of you. At times, I used to **regret** not going to school, so I made sure that my children and grandchildren studied well ...'

What does the word *avva* mean?

I could not understand why my sixty-two-year-old grandmother was telling me, a twelve-year-old, the story of her life in the middle of the night. But I knew I loved her **immensely** and there had to be some reason why she was talking to me. I looked at her face. It was unhappy and her eyes were filled with tears. She was a good-looking lady who was usually always smiling.

Even today, I cannot forget the worried expression on her face. I leaned forward and held her hand.

'*Avva*, don't cry. What is the matter? Can I help you in any way?'

'Yes, I need your help. You know, when you were away, *Karmaveera* came as usual. I opened the magazine. I saw the picture that **accompanies** the story of *Kashi Yatre* but I could not understand anything that was written. Many times, I rubbed my hands over the pages wishing I could understand what was written. But I knew it was not possible. If only I were educated enough. I waited eagerly for you to return. I felt you would come early and read for me. I even thought of going to the village and asking you to read for me. I could have asked somebody in this village but I was too **embarrassed** to do so. I felt so very dependent and helpless. We are well-off, but what use is money when I cannot be independent?'

I did not know what to answer. *Avva* continued.

'I have decided to learn the Kannada alphabet from tomorrow onwards. I will work very hard. I want to be independent.'

What did *Avva* want to learn from the next day?

essential: very important
regret: feel sad for not having done something
immensely: to a great extent, extremely
accompanies: comes with something
embarrassed: shy, uncomfortable or ashamed

'*Avva*, at this age of sixty-two you want to learn the alphabet? All your hair is grey, your hands are **wrinkled**, you wear spectacles and you work so much in the kitchen ...'

But she just smiled.

'For a good cause, if you are determined, you can overcome any **obstacle**. I will work harder than anybody else but I will do it. For learning, age is no limit.'

The next day onwards, I started my **tuition**. *Avva* was a wonderful student. The amount of homework she did was amazing. She would read, repeat, write and recite. I was her only teacher and she was my first student. Little did I know then that one day I would become a teacher of computer science and teach hundreds of students.

Then the *Dussehra* festival came as usual. My grandmother called me to the place of worship and made me sit on a stool. She gave me a gift. It was a length of fabric, to be tailored into a dress. Then she did something unusual. She bent down and touched my feet. I was surprised and taken aback. Elders never touch the feet of youngsters. We only touch the feet of gods we worship, and that of our elders and teachers. We consider it a mark of respect.

She said, 'I am touching the feet of a teacher, not my granddaughter, a teacher who taught me so well and with so much affection that I can now read any novel confidently. Now I am independent.

It is my duty to respect a teacher. Is it not written in our **scriptures** that a teacher should be respected, **irrespective** of age?'

I touched her feet in return and gave my gift to my first student. It was the novel *Kashi Yatre* by Triveni.

I knew then that my student had passed with flying colours[1].

Common idioms and proverbs

1. **with flying colours:** This idiom means to do something very well.

wrinkled: having lines or folds in skin
obstacle: anything that makes it difficult for someone to do something
tuition: teaching
scriptures: holy books
irrespective: without considering something or being influenced by it

In a Nutshell

Who the narrator and her grandmother

What The narrator taught her grandmother to read and write.

Why The grandmother felt helpless when she could not read a story.

Where a village in north Karnataka

About the author

Sudha Murty (born 1950) is an Indian author and educator, and she writes in both Kannada and English. Her stories uphold positive human values like simple living and charity. Some of her well-known works are *The Serpent's Revenge*, *The Day I Stopped Drinking Milk* and *Grandma's Bag of Stories*.

Comprehension

A. Answer the questions.

1. What did the narrator's grandmother discuss with her friends at the temple courtyard?
2. Why was a wedding an event of merriment for the children?
3. Why was the narrator's grandmother sad? What did she say about her past?
4. What kind of help did the narrator's grandmother ask for? What was the narrator's reaction to it?
5. Describe how the lessons between the narrator and her grandmother progressed.
6. How did they celebrate *Dussehra* that year?
7. What, according to the grandmother, was written in the scriptures?

B. Answer the questions as directed.

HOTS

1. Circle the options that describe *Avva*.

   a. hardworking b. traditional c. respectful d. timid

2. Complete the word using the hint.

   The narrator's grandmother felt confident and independent when she became __ I __ __ R __ __ E.

   (Hint: to be able to read and write)

3. When *Avva* was a young girl, she ________________

   1. never went to school.
   2. got married very young.
   3. did not regret going to school.

   Choose the correct option.

   a. 1 and 2 b. 2 and 3 c. 1 and 3

4. Look at the two given word pairs. They are related to each other based on a common logic. Understand it and complete the second word pair, using a suitable word from the story.

   dependent: independent :: nervously: ________________

Life Skills and Values

compassion, right to education

1. What kind of relationship did the narrator share with her grandmother? Explain using lines from the text.
2. Do you agree with Krishtakka's statement that 'For learning, age is no limit'? Explain using lines from the text.

Vocabulary

words related to books and reading

ia **A. Fill in the blanks with the given words related to books and reading.**

bookworm novels binding published plot browse

1. This book has been __________ in over forty languages.
2. My grandfather is the proud owner of old and rare books in leather __________.
3. I like to __________ through the humour section whenever I'm in a bookstore.
4. Divya is such a __________. She does not go anywhere without a book.
5. My brother loves to read mystery __________.
6. She has read the story so many times that she knows the __________ by heart.

forming antonyms with prefixes *dis-*, *un-*, *il-*

We can form antonyms or opposites by adding prefixes like *dis-*, *un-* and *il-* before words.

Examples: She was ***unhappy*** and her eyes were filled with tears.

She did not want to ***disrespect*** her teacher.

ia **B. Fill in the blanks with the antonyms of the given words. Add the prefixes *dis-*, *un-* and *il-* to form the antonyms.**

1. Sahil's room is big but __________ (tidy).
2. It does not pay to be __________ (honest).
3. __________ (legal) acts are punishable by law.
4. The magician __________ (appeared) in the blink of an eye.
5. This trek route feels quite __________ (safe).
6. The comics you are looking for have been __________ (continued).
7. The team tried to win the match by using __________ (fair) tactics.

Grammar

position of adjectives

Sometimes we have two or more adjectives before a noun in a sentence. These adjectives should be placed in a specific order for the sentence to make complete sense.

Examples: I was surprised to see **my strong, sixty-two-year-old** grandmother in tears.
She was a **jolly, good-looking old** lady who was usually always smiling.
I was her **only young** teacher, and she was my **first elderly** student.

This table shows the order in which we use adjectives.

quantity	quality	size	shape	age	colour	nationality	material	noun
ten	*fluffy*	*little*			*white*			ducklings
one		*huge*	*square*		*brown*		*wooden*	carton
many	*talented*			*young*		*Indian*		students

ia **A. Read these sentences and rewrite them using the adjectives given in brackets. Remember to position the adjectives correctly. One has been done for you.**

1. Marta and I rescued a puppy. (injured, tiny, white)
   Marta and I rescued an injured, tiny, white puppy.
2. The headmaster scolded the students who were creating most of the ruckus. (five, unruly)
3. The flowers will bloom in spring. (round, huge, orange)
4. The clouds covered the sky. (gloomy, grey, thick)
5. The explorers entered the forest. (young, African, brave, four)
6. Dara baked cookies for the guests. (lemon, round, sweet, some)

adjectives: degrees of comparison

We can compare two or more nouns using various forms of adjectives. There are three degrees of comparison of adjectives.

The basic form of an adjective, in which no comparison is made, is called the **positive degree**.

Example: *Avva* was a **wonderful** student.

When we use an adjective to compare two nouns, we use the **comparative degree** of that adjective. We use *than* after the comparative degree of an adjective.

Language Booster

We do not use *more* before an adjective that is already in the comparative degree.

Ravi is *more faster* than Shamim. ✗

Ravi is *faster* than Shamim. ✓

We form the comparative degree either by adding *-er* after the adjective or by adding the word *more* before the adjective.

Example: The narrator and her cousins were **freer** and **more talkative** than usual because all the elders were busy with the wedding.

When three or more nouns are compared based on a common quality, the **superlative degree** of the adjective is used. The article *the* is used before the superlative degree of an adjective.

We form the superlative degree either by adding *-est* after the adjective or by adding the word *most* before the adjective.

Example: *Avva* was the **most hardworking** student we had ever seen. She would forget all her work and listen with the **greatest** concentration.

ia **B. Fill in the blanks with the correct degree of comparison of the given adjectives.**

1. The streets of Mumbai are much __________ than the streets of Vadodara. (busy)
2. There was a __________ amaltas tree outside the house. (beautiful)
3. *Tom and Jerry* is the __________ animated film I have ever watched. (funny)
4. You can solve this problem both ways, but the first way is __________ than the second one. (easy)
5. Ants are one of the __________ insects. (hardworking)
6. Our science teacher is __________ than our mathematics teacher, though we enjoy being taught by both. (strict)

Study Skills

Dictionary Skills

synonyms

You know that you can use your dictionary to find synonyms of different words.

Examples: selfless: **unselfish**, **generous**
dedication: **devotion**, **commitment**

Look up the words in the dictionary and choose the correct synonym for each word.

1.	handwriting:	__________	a. scrawl	b. screech	c. scratch
2.	wrinkled:	__________	a. twinkled	b. winked	c. creased
3.	essential:	__________	a. necessary	b. useless	c. sensible
4.	respect:	__________	a. regard	b. inspect	c. disregard
5.	thoroughly:	__________	a. loudly	b. completely	c. roughly

Listening

listening for details

Listen to a passage about a woman's recollections about her grandmother and fill in the blanks.

1. The grandmother was __________ and could read __________ and __________.
2. The narrator's grandparents used to read a newspaper called __________.
3. The narrator went to India when she was __________ years old.
4. The grandmother asked her to write a __________ to her uncle.
5. The narrator's uncle's hometown was in __________.
6. The granddaughter used to call her grandmother __________.

Speaking

group discussion

Teaching or educating people is a way of serving the community. What are some other ways of helping people, especially those who are less privileged? In groups of four, think of two ways in which you can serve the community. Then, take turns to share your ideas in class, explaining how they will make a difference.

You can consider the following points:

- People: volunteering at a senior citizens' home, animal shelter, or orphanage
- Environment: raising awareness, organizing clean-up drives
- Helping out at home: reaching out to helpers, the elderly, helping with household tasks

Writing

message writing

Messages are short letters sent to communicate with people briefly. Look at this sample message.

MESSAGE

Date → 17 May 2024

Time → 7.30 a.m.

Dear Mother, ← Salutation

I will be returning late from school today, so I will not be able to join you at the mall to buy Grandpa's birthday gift. I have Kathak practice from 2 p.m. to 4 p.m. in preparation for next month's annual function. I am sorry I forgot to inform you about it earlier. ← Body

Writer → Abhilash

Imagine that you are the narrator of the story. Write a short message within 50 words to your grandmother, telling her that you have gone out to buy a novel by Triveni from the local bookseller.

Explore More

Read the book *Anne of Avonlea* by L. M. Montgomery. It is the second in the *Anne Shirley* series. It describes Anne's new life as a teacher in her old school, as she settles into Avonlea society.

Watch the 2011 film *I Am Kalam* by Nila Madhab Panda about Chotu, a poor boy with a dream to become like Dr A. P. J. Abdul Kalam, the eleventh President of India.

Listen to the speech *Education First* by Malala Yousafzai at the United Nations in 2013. This was her first speech after she survived a violent Taliban attack.

Answers to Self-Assessment

A. 1. Everyone in the class is making noise.
2. The singer and a few other musicians are organizing a special concert.
3. Each of the dancers moves beautifully.
4. Either Kabir or Faizan is going to help with the party.
5. A bouquet of yellow roses was given to the judge.

B. 1. The music is too loud for my comfort.
2. What is the poet trying to say through this poem?
3. Do not cross the street when the signal is green.
4. How melodious is the pitter-patter of the falling raindrops!
5. Please close all the doors and the windows before going out.

C. I stood on the field, shocked. Now, because of my foolish behaviour, the whole team was going to suffer. A team member should always work for the betterment the team. But what had I done? I went back to my desk and sat quietly in my chair. After thinking for a while, I knew what I should do. I took a sheet of paper and wrote my apology letter on it. I went to my coach's chamber and gave him the letter. Then I stood at the door waiting for him to read it.

D. 1. The crow flew low and dived into the water
2. We can go to the science exhibition or attend the debate.
3. We should avoid fast food because it's not healthy.
4. The cat was startled but it did not run away.
5. It wasn't safe to remain at the accident spot, so we moved to a safer place.

E. 1. rare: common
2. create: destroy
3. disagree: agree
4. major: minor
5. punish: reward

F. 1. I have been feeling weak for a week.
2. I would like two pairs of pears, please.
3. The fighting countries made peace after a piece of territory was handed over.
4. The knight arrived at the castle last night.
5. Some tribes pray before hunting their prey.

non-fiction

4

Children of India

Ruskin Bond

Curricular Goals

- develop a comprehensive range of vocabulary in various contexts
- understand basic linguistic aspects such as tense, sentence structure and parts of speech
- listen critically and paraphrase ideas
- write different kinds of letters in appropriate style for different audiences and purposes

Competencies

- can use commonly confused words and phrasal verbs correctly
- can identify subject and predicate, and the different types of tenses
- can participate in a debate and write a formal letter

Reading

a *How do you go to school – by bus, car, auto or on foot? There are many children in our country who overcome various obstacles daily to reach their schools. Read on to find out how they deal with such situations and come out winners.*

INDIA FOCUS

They pass me every day, on their way to school – boys and girls from the surrounding villages and the **outskirts** of the hill station. There are no school buses **plying** for these children. For many of them, it's a very long walk to school. Ranbir, who is ten, has to climb the mountain from his village, four miles distant and two thousand feet below the town level. He comes in all weathers, wearing the same pair of cheap shoes until they have almost fallen apart.

How far is Ranbir's village from the school?

Ranbir is a cheerful soul. He waves to me whenever he sees me at my window. Sometimes he brings cucumbers from his father's field. I pay him for the cucumbers; he uses the money for books or for small things needed at home.

Many of the children are like Ranbir – poor, but slightly better off than what their parents were at the same age. They cannot attend the expensive residential and private schools that **abound** here, but most go to the government-aided schools with only basic facilities. Not many

outskirts: the parts of a town or city that are farthest from the centre

plying: travelling regularly on a particular route

abound: exist in great numbers

of their parents managed to go to school. They spent their lives working in the fields or delivering milk in the hill station. The lucky ones got into the army. Perhaps Ranbir will do something different when he grows up. He has yet to see a train but he sees planes flying over the mountains almost every day.

Cross-curricular Corner

Winters are severe in the hills, with heavy snowfall making it impossible for people to come out of their homes for several days. They not only have to store enough food for themselves but also for their animals. They usually do this before winter, when plants have not dried up yet.

'How far can a plane go?' he asks.

'All over the world,' I tell him. 'Thousands of miles in a day. You can go almost anywhere.'

'I'll go round the world one day,' he vows. 'I'll buy a plane and go everywhere!' And maybe he will. He has a determined chin and a **defiant** look in his eye. These lines in my journal were put down for my own inspiration or encouragement, but they will do for any determined young person. We get out of life what we bring to it. There is not a dream which may not come true if we have the energy which determines our own fate. We can always get what we want if we will it **intensely** enough … it may come when we no longer have any use of it, but if we have been willing it long enough, it will come!

Up to a few years ago, very few girls in the hills or in the villages of India went to school. They helped in the home until they were old enough to be married, which wasn't very old. But there are now just as many girls as there are boys going to school.

Bindra is something of an **extrovert**, a confident fourteen-year-old who chatters away as she hurries down the road with her companions. Her father is a forest guard and knows me quite well: I meet him on my walks through the *deodar* woods behind Landour. And I had grown used to seeing Bindra almost

defiant: bold, aggressive
intensely: strongly

extrovert: a lively and confident person who enjoys being with others every day. When she did not put in an appearance[1] for a week, I asked her brother if anything was wrong.

'Oh, nothing,' he says, 'she is helping my mother cut grass. Soon the monsoon will end and the grass will dry up. So we cut it now and store it for the cows in winter.'

'And why aren't you cutting grass too?'

'Oh, I have a cricket match today,' he says, and hurries away to join his teammates. Unlike his sister, he puts pleasure before work!

Common idioms and proverbs

1. **put in an appearance:** This idiom means to visit or appear at some place for some time.

Cricket, once the game of the **elite**, has become the game of the **masses**. On any holiday, in any part of this vast country, groups of boys can be seen working their way to the nearest field, or open patch of land, with bat, ball and any other cricketing **gear** that they can **cobble together**. Watching some of them play, I am amazed at the quality of talent, at the **finesse** with which they bat or bowl. Some of the local teams are as good, if not better, than any from the private schools, where there are better facilities. But the boys from these poor or lower middle-class families will never get the **exposure** that is necessary to bring them to the attention of those who select state or national teams. They will never get near enough to the men of influence and power. They must continue to play for the love of the game, to watch their more fortunate heroes' **exploits** on television.

As winter approaches and the days grow shorter, those children who live far away must quicken their pace in order to get home before dark. Ranbir and his friends find that darkness has fallen before they are halfway home.

'What is the time, Uncle?' he asks, as he **trudges** up the **steep** road past *Ivy Cottage*. One gets used to being called 'Uncle' by almost every boy or girl one meets. I wonder how the custom began. Perhaps it has its origins in the folktale about the tiger who wouldn't pounce on you if you called him 'Uncle'. Tigers don't eat their relatives! Or do they? The ploy may not work if the tiger happens to be a tigress. Would you call her 'Aunty' as she (or your teacher!) **descends** on you?

elite: a small group of people in a society who are powerful and have a lot of influence

masses: the ordinary people

gear: the equipment or clothing needed for a particular activity

cobble together: produce something quickly and without great care or effort, so that it can be used, but is not perfect

finesse: great skill

exposure: coming into contact with influential people and institutions

exploits: brave, exciting or interesting acts

trudges: walks slowly with heavy steps

steep: sharply rising, not gradual

descends: arrives unexpectedly to see someone

It's dark at six and by then, Ranbir likes to be out of the deodar forest and on the open road to the village. The moon and the stars and the village lights are sufficient, but not in the forest, where it is dark even during the day. And the silent **flitting** of bats and **flying foxes**, and the **eerie** hoot of an owl, can be a little unsettling for the **hardiest** of children. Once, Ranbir and the other boys were chased by a bear.

When he told me about it, I said, 'Well, now we know you can run faster than a bear!'

'Yes, but you have to run downhill when chased by a bear.' He spoke as one having long experience of escaping from bears. 'They run much faster uphill!'

'I'll remember that,' I said, 'thanks for the advice.' And I don't suppose calling a bear 'Uncle' would help.

Usually Ranbir has the company of other boys, and they sing most of the way, for loud singing by small boys will silence owls and frighten away the forest demons. One of them plays a flute, and flute music in the mountains is always enchanting.

Not only in the hills, but all over India, children are constantly making their way to and from school, in conditions that range from dust storms in the Rajasthan desert to **blizzards** in Ladakh and Kashmir. In the larger towns and cities, there are school buses, but in **remote** rural areas, getting to school can pose a problem.

Most children are more than equal to any obstacles that may arise. Like those youngsters in the Ganjam district of Odisha. In the absence of a bridge, they swim or **wade** across the Dhanei river every day in order to

Name the house where the author lived.

flitting: swift and light movement
flying foxes: large fruit bats
eerie: strange and frightening
hardiest: the strongest and most resourceful
blizzards: snowstorms with very strong winds
remote: far away from places where people live
wade: walk with an effort through water or mud

reach their school. I have a picture of them in my scrapbook. Holding books or **satchels aloft** in one hand, they do the breast stroke or dog paddle with the other; or form a chain and help each other across.

Wherever you go in India, you will find children helping out with the family's source of livelihood, whether it be drying fish on the Malabar coast, or gathering saffron buds in Kashmir, or grazing camels or cattle in a village in Rajasthan or Gujarat. Only the more fortunate can afford to send their children to English medium private or 'public schools', and those children really *are* fortunate, for some of these institutions are excellent schools, as good, and often better, than their **counterparts** in Britain or the USA. Whether it's in Ajmer or Bengaluru, New Delhi or Chandigarh, Kanpur or Kolkata, the best schools set very high standards.

Cross-curricular Corner

The Malabar coast is the southwestern coast of India that runs along the states of Goa, Karnataka, Kerala and Tamil Nadu.

Saffron is a spice that comes from the violet saffron crocus flower, in the form of bright red threads that add colour and flavour to food.

The great majority of our children will attend schools run by the state or **municipality**. These vary from good to the bad to the ugly, depending on how they are run and where they are situated.

A classroom without windows, or with a roof that lets in the monsoon rain, is not uncommon. Even so, children from different communities learn to live and grow together. Hardship makes brothers of us all.

The **census** tells us that two in every five of the population is in the age group of five to fifteen. Almost half our population is on the way to school!

And here I stand at my window, watching some of them pass by – boys and girls, big and small, some **scruffy**, some smart, some mischievous, some serious, but all *going* somewhere – hopefully towards a better future.

satchels: bags carried on the shoulder by long straps and closed by a flap

aloft: high in the air

counterparts: people or things closely resembling another

municipality: (in India) an urban area with a population of more than 10 lakh, with its own local government

census: an official count of the population

scruffy: shabby and untidy

In a Nutshell

Who the author and the children in his neighbourhood

What The author watches them go to school.

Why He is inspired by their inner strength and confidence.

Where Landour, Uttarakhand

About the author

Ruskin Bond (born 1934) is an Indian author of British origin. He has written many books for children as well as adults. He is best known for his short stories set in Himalayan towns. Some of his most-loved stories are *The Blue Umbrella*, *Harold the Hornbill* and *Tiger in the Tunnel*.

Comprehension

ia **A. Read the sentences in each set and tick [✓] the ones that are correct.**

HOTS

1. a. Ranbir walks four miles to reach school because he enjoys walking. [ ]
   b. Ranbir walks four miles to reach school because he has no other choice. [ ]
   c. Ranbir walks four miles to reach school because he likes chatting with his friends on the way. [ ]
2. a. Breast stroke and dog paddle are ways of walking. [ ]
   b. Breast stroke and dog paddle are ways of swimming. [ ]
   c. Breast stroke and dog paddle are methods of holding things and walking in the river. [ ]
3. a. If Ranbir were of his parents' generation, he would be going to school. [ ]
   b. If Ranbir were of his parents' generation, he would be working in the fields or delivering milk. [ ]
   c. If Ranbir were of his parents' generation, he would be in the army. [ ]
4. a. During grass-cutting season, girls are expected to miss school and help while boys are not. [ ]
   b. During grass-cutting season, girls and boys are expected to miss school and help. [ ]
   c. During grass-cutting season, boys are expected to miss school and help while girls are not. [ ]
5. By 'all going somewhere', the author means that
   a. all the children are working to reach somewhere in their lives. [ ]
   b. all the children are going to school. [ ]
   c. all the children are going to explore the world. [ ]

B. Answer the questions in a few lines.

1. How does Ranbir come across as determined while going to school?
2. Why does Ranbir like to be out of the deodar forest by 6 p.m.?
3. What picture does the author have in his scrapbook? Why do you think he has kept the picture?
4. How do the children from the Malabar coast and Kashmir help their family earn a livelihood? What does it tell us about the different types of childhood children in India have?
5. What quality of the children shines through in the story?
   a. their passion to study
   b. their intolerance of hardships
   c. their ambition

Life Skills and Values

gender equality, love for sport

Critical Thinking

1. What do you think of the difference in treatment between Bindra and her brother in the way they balance household duties, studies and play?
2. 'Hardship makes brothers of us all.' Do you agree with the author? Explain your answer with examples from the passage.
3. What does the author feel about the popularity of cricket in India? Why does he say that the boys in the hills must continue to play for the love of the game, and not for any gains or glories?

Vocabulary

commonly confused words

A. Choose the correct words to complete the sentences.

1. This dress is a little ______________ (lose/loose) for me.
2. I ran into Hema's ______________ (elder/older) brother at the mall.
3. Is ______________ (there/their) anything I can do to help you?
4. Please ______________ (accept/except) the invitation to the opening night of the play.
5. The people living in the hills were badly ______________ (effected/affected) by the landslides.
6. After the three-course meal, we still had room for ______________ (desert/dessert).

phrasal verbs

B. Several phrasal verbs like *got into* and *help out* have been used in the chapter. Fill in the blanks with the correct phrasal verbs.

put up   fell apart   gave up   put in   put down   passed by

1. He ______________ his thoughts and ideas in a secret diary.
2. Roy ______________ his position as the captain of the football team after they lost the final game.
3. The friends ______________ over a petty quarrel.
4. The actor's convoy of cars ______________ our house today.
5. All the children ______________ a lot of effort for the exhibition.
6. She ______________ with all the trouble created by the puppy.

Grammar

subject and predicate

Read these sentences.

<u>Ranbir</u> *is a cheerful soul.*

<u>Cricket</u> *has become the game of the masses.*

A sentence has two parts – a subject and a predicate. Here, the underlined words, *Ranbir* and *cricket*, are the subjects and the remaining parts of the sentences are the predicates.

The **subject** of a sentence tells us who or what the sentence is about. The **predicate** has a verb and tells us something about the subject.

To identify the subject in a sentence, we find the verb and ask *who* or *what* does the action.

Who is a cheerful soul? (=Ranbir)
What is the game of the masses? (=cricket)

ia **A. Circle the subjects and underline the predicates in the sentences.**

1. Rohan is a bright and cheerful boy.
2. My sister has two pet rabbits.
3. Tigers are endangered animals.
4. Parul and her brother are both swimming champions.
5. I met my cousins recently.
6. We want to play a game of hide-and-seek now.

tenses: simple and continuous

You know that tenses cover three aspects of time – the past, the present and the future. Each tense can be categorised into further types.

The **simple present tense** is used to talk about things that happen regularly or are universal truths. We use the base form of the verb for the simple present tense. If the subject of the sentence is in the third person and singular, we add *-s* to the verb.

Example: Bindra's brother **puts** pleasure before work.

The **present continuous tense** is used to describe a continuous or an ongoing action in the present time. It takes the form *am/are/is* + verb + *-ing*.

Example: She **is helping** my mother cut grass.

The **simple past tense** is used to refer to actions that were completed before the time of speaking. It is usually formed by adding *-d* or *-ed* to the base form of the verb.

Example: I **asked** her brother if anything was wrong.

The **past continuous tense** is used to talk about actions that went on for some time in the past. It takes the form *was/were* + verb + *-ing*.

Example: Ranbir **was wearing** the same pair of cheap shoes.

The **simple future tense** is used for actions that will happen at some point of time in the future. It takes the form, *will* + verb.

Example: I **will buy** a plane and go everywhere.

The **future continuous tense** is used for actions that will start in the future and continue for some time. It takes the form *will be* + verb + *-ing*.

Example: Soon, the monsoon **will be ending**.

ia **B. Fill in the blanks with the correct options to complete Haroon's diary entry about a trip to an amusement park.**

Dear Diary,

Summer vacations __________ (begin/began) yesterday. My friends, Karim, Vibha, Tarun, and I __________ (will go/were going) to the amusement park the day after tomorrow. Every year, we __________ (visit/visited) the zoo during our vacations, but this year we __________ (are deciding/decided) to do something different. Everyone __________ (will gather/are gathering) at my house. Then we __________ (will take/take) a taxi to the park. My parents __________ (will be coming/ were coming) along to look after us. I __________ (plan/planned) to go on all the rides, even the scariest ones. This afternoon, I __________ (am watching/was watching) a video of a ride in the park, in which the people __________ (hang/hung) upside down at a great height in their seats. Everyone in the video __________ (was screaming/screamed). I __________ (feel/felt) scared but also thrilled. After the amusement park, all of us __________ (will go/went) to Vibha's house and have dinner there. I am so excited!

Study Skills

Spelling

names of professions using *-er, -ian, -ist*

Look at these words.

cricket**er** music**ian** journal**ist**

These are names of professions formed by adding suffixes like *-er, -ian* and *-ist* to the base words *cricket, music* and *journal* respectively.

Fill in the blanks with suitable names of professions, formed by adding *-er, -ian* and *-ist* to suitable base words.

1. The ______________ painted the doors and windows white.
2. The ______________ thrilled the audience with his disappearing tricks.
3. We had to call the ______________ to replace the bulbs and lights.
4. The ______________ has discovered a cure for the deadly disease.
5. The ______________ had a barn full of cattle and horses.
6. The ______________ took the infected tooth out neatly.

Listening

listening for information

Listen to a passage about volunteering at a wildlife sanctuary. Then write whether the following statements are true (T) or false (F).

1. The narrator worked at a wildlife sanctuary in South America. ☐
2. More than a hundred animals lived there. ☐
3. The narrator once had breakfast while a baboon sat next to her. ☐
4. Lions and leopards roamed freely in the sanctuary. ☐
5. The narrator enjoyed bathing the baby animals the most. ☐
6. There were meerkats, mongooses, porcupines, tortoises and deer. ☐

Speaking

debate (financial literacy)

21st Century: Communication; Information Literacy

In the story you read about children who come from financial backgrounds. Do you think saving and investing money is important? Work in two groups and have a debate in class on the topic, with one group speaking in favour of the topic and the other against it. You can use the following points, and add your own:

For

- Saving money helps us to be prepared for unexpected emergencies.
- It also helps us invest and increase our money for future expenses.

Against

- It is better to spend money in order to live a comfortable life.
- We miss out on a good life if we focus only on saving money.

Writing

formal letter

21st Century: Initiative

You are the school representative of Hills Public School, Dehradun. An avalanche struck your neighbourhood two weeks ago, blocking the road to the school. All the students are facing difficulties in commuting, with many of them having to pass through the forest, risking encounters with wild animals. Write a letter to the Municipal Commissioner informing them about the situation and requesting for the road to be repaired.

Explore More

Read the book *Oliver Twist* by Charles Dickens, about an orphan boy who survives in various difficult situations because of his sheer determination.

Watch the film *Nil Battey Sannata* (*The New Classmate*), directed by Ashwin Iyer Tiwari. It is about a poor teenaged girl, who wants to give up studying because of her social and financial conditions, but is inspired by her mother to continue.

Listen to the song 'Touch the Sky' by Julie Fowlis, from the Disney film *Brave*. It celebrates the main character's fearlessness and determination to do as she wishes.

UNIT III

Nature and Conservation

Warm-up

A. The United Nations Sustainable Development Goal 15 states that we must stop the loss of forest and green cover, and the species which live in them.

Work in pairs to see who completes the grid the fastest in class. Read the clues for some medicinal trees and plants in India and write their names.

1. This tree has bitter leaves. Its hard stem has been traditionally used for cleaning teeth.
2. This tall evergreen tree is known for its oil. It is used traditionally for cough and cold, and as an insect repellent.
3. This plant is grown in the courtyards of many Indian homes. It has medicinal properties.
4. The yellow powder made from its roots is used as a common spice.
5. The fruit from this tree is used in Goan and Maharashtrian cuisine to add a sour taste to dishes.
6. This is the national tree of India.

1. _ E _ M	2. E _ C _ L _ P _ U _	3. _ U _ S _
4. T _ R _ E _ I _	5. K _ K _ M	6. B _ N _ A _

B. The United Nations Sustainable Development Goal 13 states that we must take action to deal with climate change by controlling pollution. People across the world are struggling to deal with the effects of climate change and global warming. Write down six ways in which you see nature around you being harmfully affected by human activity.

short story

5

An Old Friend

Jayanti Adhikari

Curricular Goals

- develop a comprehensive range of vocabulary in various contexts
- recognize basic linguistic aspects and use them
- ability to communicate effectively using language skills for description, analysis, and response
- write prose, poetry and drama by using appropriate language

→

Competencies

- can use words in the text contextually
- can apply the concept of agreement of subject and verb, and use punctuation correctly
- can spell *ie* and *ei* words correctly
- can conduct an interview, write a story

Reading

a *How do you feel when you are surrounded by trees and plants? Have you ever planted a tree yourself? Read this tale of friendship between a boy and a neem tree that his grandfather had planted.*

INDIA FOCUS

Shyamal was looking **affectionately** at the neem tree from his bed. He had been in bed with typhoid for a month and Nimai had been his companion through that time. He could hardly think of a more comforting sight than the handsome and elegant tree **holding** its **head high**[1] against the background of the blue sky. He could almost hear his grandfather's voice in the **murmur** of the small green leaves and the long, spreading branches. Grandfather would often tell him how people believed that a few drops of heavenly **nectar** fell on the neem tree, giving it medicinal properties.

Shyamal's grandfather had planted the neem tree on the day their family came to live in the newly built house. Although Shyamal was not born at that time, he imagined his young grandfather entering the house, smiling proudly. In his hand was the neem plant, which he had collected from the old gardener in his office.

Since then, Nimai, as the tree was named, had been a part of their lives. It was the place for Grandfather's morning prayers. The neighbourhood remembered his gentle, rhythmic voice chanting the ***surya pranam***. In summer, he would come

Literary term

1. This is an example of **personification**. The tree is imagined to be a person holding his head up with pride.

affectionately: in a way that shows fondness
holding head high: being proud and confident in one's conduct
murmur: a continuous low sound
nectar: a liquid which the gods drink
surya pranam: a Sanskrit chant devoted to the sun god, Surya

and sit under the tree as the afternoon breeze started. How he loved to see the neem flowers appearing from March to April, the air carrying their light **fragrance** and the greenish-yellow fruits ripening from June to August. For hours, he would sit there reading, writing, or gazing at the young leaves, and the birds and squirrels who lived in it.

He could talk endlessly about the uses of every part of the tree. The seed oil and soap could be used for various skin diseases. The bark was used as **tincture**. Shyamal's grandmother always kept dried neem leaves in between books and clothes to protect them from **weevils**. A favourite family dish was neem leaves fried with small pieces of brinjal.

In his childhood, Grandfather had once had smallpox. Grandfather's mother used to comfort his burning skin with the feather light touch of neem leaves. He often told Shyamal, his most devoted listener, that the neem leaves still reminded him of his mother's affectionate touch. Shyamal always remembered the day the news came of Grandmother's sudden death while she was at his uncle's house in Mysore. The old man didn't utter a word, but sat all day under the tree, perhaps looking at his age-old companion for strength.

Grandfather left their family just as suddenly and silently. Shyamal had been sent to call Grandfather, who had been sitting under the neem tree all evening, inside. At first, Shyamal had thought he was **dozing** and had tried to wake him up. 'Grandfather, your time of chatting with Nimai is up.'

But the old man's head fell to his chest at Shyamal's touch. As Shyamal stood, shocked, he noticed a few dried neem leaves **flutter** down to Grandfather's lap.

That had been a few months ago. Shyamal was a thoughtful boy. The loss had affected him deeply. This afternoon, he was lost in his thoughts[2], looking at Nimai's shiny leaves. His mother came in with the news of the day. 'The new car your father talked about will be delivered this evening.' This was great news indeed, and the boy was very excited. He jumped down from his bed and announced, 'I am not going to stay in bed anymore. This very evening, I am going on a long drive with Papa.'

Common idioms and phrases

2. **to be lost in one's thoughts:** This phrase means concentrating on one's thoughts so much that you don't notice what is happening around you.

When the first rush of excitement was over, his mother broke the next piece of news to Shyamal **cautiously**, 'Your father says that we have to cut down Nimai to make place for a garage for the car.' Shyamal could not believe his ears.

'How can you do that? Would you get rid of me because of lack of space? Don't you remember how much Grandpa loved the tree?' The fourteen-year-old boy's voice was lost in sobs.

Shyamal's mother called his father. There was a long argument between father and son on the phone, but the boy would not **budge**.

Why did Shyamal's father plan to cut down Nimai?

fragrance: a sweet smell
tincture: a substance dissolved in alcohol for use as a medicine
weevils: small insects which feed on grain and seeds, and destroy crops
dozing: sleeping
flutter: move through the air with small, quick movements
cautiously: carefully
budge: (here) change his opinion or come to an agreement

'You are just being stubborn, son. Your grandfather was my father. I loved him too. We can remember him in a hundred other ways. Where else can we keep the car?' his father asked. In the end, he announced that the woodcutters would come the next morning, whether Shyamal liked it or not.

Shyamal was left to himself for the rest of the day. The house was busy, and nobody seemed to notice the **morose** boy. Towards the evening, the sky was dark with heavy rain clouds. There was a **clap of thunder** and big drops of rain started to fall. The fragrance of wet soil reminded Shyamal of his grandfather and the way he took in deep breaths of the rain-soaked air.

Suddenly, there was a deafening sound. The lights in the house went off and a bright flash lit up the world outside for a second. When his eyes adjusted themselves to the darkness, Shyamal saw that Nimai was burning and heard his father scream from somewhere near the gate. This was too much for the boy, who had been a **bundle of nerves** from the feared loss of his beloved tree. His head spun as he sank to the ground.

When he opened his eyes, he saw his family looking at him. His father held him in his arms. There were tears in his eyes. Later, they told him that a big bolt of lightning had struck the tree. Had it not been for Nimai, it would have struck his father as he got out from the car. Even as the tree died, it performed a last act of kindness for the family.

The next morning, Shyamal was not in his room. A note on his table said that he was going out with their old helper, Prasad.

As the day wore on[3], his parents got more and more anxious. Shyamal's father, his uncles and friends went out to search for him at his friends' homes, and then in hospitals and police stations. But there was no news to be had. The fourteen-year-old boy and the old servant seemed to have vanished from the city.

Common idioms and phrases

3. **as the day wore on:** This phrase means 'as the day passed by slowly'.

It was almost 10:30 at night. The lights **blazed** in every room. The **extended family** filled the house, but nobody spoke. Suddenly, somebody shouted, 'There he is!' Everyone rushed out. Shyamal could be seen at a distance, followed by Prasad. The boy had walked a long way. His face **gleamed** with sweat, and dust covered his knees. But his face was lit up with a triumphant smile. He held a small neem sapling in his hands. Everybody began questioning him at once, but he only answered his mother.

'Ma, I found Grandfather's old gardener's house with the help of Prasad uncle. Now, this sapling will take Nimai's place.'

Where did Shyamal go with Prasad?

His face shone with the love which his grandfather had passed on to him.

morose: sad and easy to anger

clap of thunder: the deep rumbling sound heard in the sky after a flash of lightning

bundle of nerves: very nervous

blazed: lit up too brightly

extended family: a family group that includes relatives such as uncles, aunts and grandparents, besides parents and children

gleamed: shone

In a Nutshell

Who Shyamal, his parents and grandfather, and Nimai, the neem tree

What Shyamal's love for the neem tree

Why It reminded him of his beloved grandfather, who had loved the tree and had taught Shyamal to appreciate it.

Comprehension

HOTS

A. Choose the correct option.

1. Which of the following things would Grandfather do with Nimai?
   a. He would say his morning prayers.
   b. He would play the sitar.
   c. He would sit under it, reading or writing.
2. *'... Would you get rid of me because of lack of space?'*
   What did Shyamal mean by this question?
   a. His parents did not love Shyamal as much as the new car.
   b. His parents should see Nimai as family, just like Shyamal.
   c. His parents should find a new place for Nimai.
3. Shyamal felt that Nimai had been his <u>companion</u> when he was ill with typhoid.
   Which of the following words cannot replace the underlined word?
   a. friend
   b. partner
   c. playmate
4. *'You are just being stubborn, son.'*
   Which word describes Shyamal's father's reaction?
   a. considerate
   b. unkind
   c. affectionate
5. *'Ma, I found Grandfather's old gardener's house with the help of Prasad uncle. Now, this sapling will take Nimai's place.'*
   What do you understand from this line? You can choose more than one option.
   a. Shyamal's love for his grandfather. ☐
   b. Shyamal's connection with Nimai. ☐
   c. Shyamal is a determined and hardworking boy. ☐

B. Answer the questions in a few lines.

1. Describe the friendship between Shyamal's grandfather and Nimai using examples from the story.
2. How do you think Shyamal felt when his grandfather died? Do you think Shyamal's love towards Nimai was because of his grandfather?
3. What was Nimai's last act of kindness?
4. What was the situation at Shyamal's house through the day after he left home?
5. What do you think of the fact that Shyamal's father was saved by the very tree he wanted to cut down?

Life Skills and Values

caring about nature, civic values

1. The friendship between a tree and a human being is a bond that does not need any exchange of words. What do you think of the title of the story with reference to this statement?
2. Do you think Shyamal's grandfather felt lonely after his wife passed away? Support your answer with lines from the story. Suggest ways in which you can make your grandparents or other elderly members of the family feel loved and cared for.

Vocabulary

contextual usage

Fill in the blanks with these words from the story.

morose sapling deafening rhythmic tincture anxious

1. The __________ tunes brought everyone to the dance floor.
2. The __________ noise of a tyre bursting made the passers-by stop in their tracks.
3. The __________ I planted with my father did not survive the extreme winter.
4. Iodine __________ is a common antiseptic used to prevent infection from cuts and burns.
5. The passengers felt __________ because of the delay in the flight's landing.
6. Rahim tried to cheer his __________ nephew up by taking him for a swim.

Grammar

agreement of subject and verb

You have learnt that for a sentence to be grammatically correct, the main verb should agree with the subject in person and number. This is called the **agreement of the subject and verb.**

Look at some of the rules of subject–verb agreement.

- When the subject is singular, the verb should be singular. When the subject is plural, the verb is also plural.
  Example: Your father **says** that we have to cut down Nimai.
- Two or more subjects joined by *and* take a plural verb.
  Example: Shyamal and his grandfather **were** very close.
- If a subject comes after *each* or *every*, the verb is usually singular. The same rule applies to pronouns like *anyone*, *anybody*, *no one*, *nobody*, *someone* and *somebody*.
  Examples: There isn't anyone who **knows** as much about trees as Shyamal's grandfather.
  No one **knows** where Shyamal has vanished.
- When the subject is made up of two or more nouns joined by conjunctions like *either … or, neither … nor*, the verb agrees with the noun or pronoun that is placed closest to it.
  Examples: Neither Shyamal nor his mother **wants** Nimai to be cut down.
  Either Shyamal or his parents **are going** to Mysuru this year.

ia **A. Fill in the blanks with the correct options.**

1. Bread, butter and eggs ______________ (is/are) common breakfast items.
2. Each of the soldiers ______________ (has/have) shown tremendous bravery.
3. Somebody ______________ (is/are) coming to repair the fridge.
4. The cow and the horses ______________ (was/were) grazing on the field.
5. Neither Rehaan nor Urja ______________ (has/have) arrived yet.
6. No one in the playground ______________ (is/are) is playing football today.

punctuation

The most commonly used punctuation marks are the full stop (.), the comma (,), the question mark (?), the exclamation mark (!) and quotation marks(').

A **full stop** is used to indicate a long pause. We use it when we want to end a statement or a command.

A **comma** is used to indicate a very short pause.

A **question mark** is used at the end of a question.

An **exclamation mark** is used at the end of a sentence which shows strong feelings such as happiness, sadness and anger.

We use **quotation marks** or inverted commas to indicate the exact words of the speaker in direct speech.

Quotation marks show the beginning and the end of the actual words of the speaker.

We add a comma (,) before the closing quotation mark if the words in direct speech is a sentence. We omit it if the words form a question or end in an exclamation mark.

Examples: 'I am not going to stay in bed anymore,' thought Shyamal.
Suddenly, somebody shouted, 'There he is!'
'How can you do that?'

Language Booster

The first word of the sentence within quotation marks begins with a capital letter.

Example: The father said, 'You are being stubborn, son.'

ia **B. Rewrite these sentences with the correct punctuation marks.**

1. what a delicious dish
2. what was the result of the match
3. let us go for a walk
4. sherlock holmes lived in london
5. amit said to gurshabad turn all the lights off before leaving
6. please pack my pink dress white hat sunglasses and blue slippers
7. have you seen my brown suitcase anywhere

Study Skills

Spelling

ie and *ei* words

Look at these words.

piece believe friend

In most words with the letters *i* and *e*, *i* is usually placed before *e*. But there are exceptions where we spell the words with *ei*.

Examples: neighbourhood being their

Read the meanings and complete the words by adding *ei* or *ie*.

1. n_ _ghbour: a person living next door
2. f_ _ld: an area of land
3. for_ _gn: of another country
4. pr_ _st: someone who performs religious duties
5. rec_ _ve: get something
6. h_ _ght: measurement from head to toe
7. ach_ _ve: succeed in doing something

Listening

listening for information

Listen to a passage on the neem tree and write whether these statements are true (T) or false (F).

1. Neem is known as the 'world's dispensary'. ☐
2. Neem is used to cure cough, cold and diabetes. ☐
3. Neem is a deciduous tree belonging to the mahogany family. ☐
4. It has small flowers that smell like honey and attract bees. ☐
5. Neem trees are hardy and can grow in harsh conditions. ☐
6. Neem oil is used in soaps, shampoos and lotions. ☐

Dictation

You will now listen to a short story about Tenali Raman. Write it down. Each sentence will be repeated twice. Listen carefully and be careful not to make any spelling errors.

Speaking

conversation: asking for suggestions

21ST CENTURY Media Literacy · 21ST CENTURY Communication

You are the head of the school's radio club. Imagine that a famous environmentalist is visiting your school. In pairs, enact a conversation with him/her asking for suggestions on what we can do to stop our neighbourhoods from becoming concrete jungles.

You may use the following points:

- importance of trees
- why he/she thinks those who cut down trees do not fear the harmful effects it would have on their own future generations

Useful words and phrases

- What can we ...
- Do you think ...
- Is there a way
- Perhaps we could ...

Writing

writing a story

21ST CENTURY Creativity

In the story, Shyamal's father wanted to cut down Nimai, but his life is saved by the tree. Using the given clues, write a story about a person who begins to care for the environment after an impactful incident. Your story should have a logical plot, well-developed characters and an interesting ending.

northern forests drying up – villagers living close to the northern mountains scared – fear forest fires, droughts and landslides – new district collector posted to the area – city man who doesn't care about the environment – meets villagers who show him the many ways the forest helps them survive – change of heart – starts working to save the forests

Explore More

Read the story, 'The Cherry Tree' by Ruskin Bond, about a small boy who plants a cherry seed and takes care of the plant as it grows into a tree over the next three years.

Watch the 2012 animated film *The Lorax* directed by Chris Renaud about the plight of the environment. The main character, Lorax, is the protector of the forest and speaks on behalf of the trees.

Listen to the 2019 speech by teen-activist Greta Thunberg at the United Nations Climate Action Summit. It is about the dangers of climate change in which she holds world leaders accountable for their actions.

6 Progress Man

Judith Nicholls

Curricular Goals

- develop a comprehensive range of vocabulary in different contexts
- able to use language effectively in other curricular areas

→

Competencies

- can understand and apply the concept of compound nouns, and can use homonyms in sentences
- can complete a fact sheet

Reading

a *The harmful effects of climate change, from hotter temperatures and wildfires to declining population of wildlife, are making headlines every other day. What is the most recent news you have read on climate change? Read this poem that sheds light on the cause of this alarming situation – reckless human activities.*

Hurry now! *cried* ***Progress***[1],
just see what I can do!
Watch my **chain-saw**, feel my axe;
my ways are great for you,

'cos I'm a ***swinging****, singing*[2],
Racing, ***chasing****,* do-it-how-I-can,
I'm the swinging, singing,
Racing, chasing Progress Man!

See me chop your forests down,
we need a **motorway**!
You have some roads already ...?
Well, not enough I say,

and I'm a swinging, singing,
racing, chasing, do-it-how-I-can,
I'm the swinging, singing,
Racing, chasing Progress Man!

progress: growth, improvement, development

chain-saw: a big battery-powered saw with a rotating chain and metallic teeth

swinging: making something move with a wide curved movement (referring to an axe)

chasing: trying very hard to get something one wants

motorway: a huge road with several lanes for fast travel over long distances

Literary term

1. This is an example of **personification**. The concept of progress is represented as a person.

What's a little drop of oil
spilt over golden sand?
It's just a tiny price to pay,
the world has so much land,

and I'm a swinging, singing,
racing, chasing, do-it-how-I-can,
I'm the swinging, singing,
Racing, chasing Progress Man!

In a Nutshell

Who the 'Progress Man', who represents industrial development

What harmful effects of cutting down trees and drilling oil for progress

Where all over the world

About the poet

Judith Nicholls (born 1941) is a former teacher and English poet, best known for writing poetry for children. She has published over 50 books. Her notable works include *Caliban's Cave* and *The Sun in Me.*

Understanding the Poem

HOTS

A. Choose the correct answers.

1. What does Progress Man mean by the line 'my ways are great for you'?
   a. His actions are quick and beneficial for humans.
   b. His actions are beneficial for the environment.
   c. Both *a* and *b* are correct.
2. What do the lines 'You have some roads already...? / Well, not enough, I say,' imply?
   a. Humans love building roads.
   b. Humans are greedy and are never satisfied.
   c. Those who want to become rich by building roads try to make us believe that we need them.
3. The line 'What's a little drop of oil / spilt over golden sand?' refers to
   a. oil spills in the oceans.
   b. drops of oil on the beach.
   c. oil in the desert.
4. The line 'It's just a tiny price to pay, the world has so much land.' suggests that
   a. land is cheap, so more can be bought if one area is damaged.
   b. it doesn't matter if a part of the world is damaged for the sake of progress.
   c. there are many places to live in this world.
5. The tone of the poem is
   a. cheery.
   b. angry.
   c. funny.

B. Answer these questions in a few lines.

1. Why does Progress Man cry 'Hurry now!'?
2. What does Progress Man mean when he says that he is a 'do-it-how-I-can' type of person?
3. Why do you think the concept of progress is imagined as a person?
4. The poem repeats a stanza thrice. Why do you think it is repeated?

Life Skills and Values

social responsibility, critical analysis

21ST CENTURY Critical Thinking

1. Progress is important for human civilization, but the way it is achieved matters even more. Do you agree?
2. In the poem, the speaker, Progress Man sounds happy and cheerful. Do you feel happy after reading the poem? Why/why not? Discuss in class.

Vocabulary

compound nouns

A **compound noun** is formed by combining two or more nouns to make a completely new word. The meaning of the new word is usually different from that of its parts.

The two nouns in the compound noun may be hyphenated, joined together, or separated by a space.

Examples: 'Watch my **chain-saw**, feel my axe;' (chain + saw)

'We need a **motorway**!' (motor + way)

Mohan bought a new **washing machine**. (washing + machine)

ia **A. Complete the sentences by forming compound nouns from the words in the box.**

chop	rail	air	life	port	book
post	time	note	office	sticks	way

1. The ________________ station was extremely crowded.
2. I saw her at the ________________ today, near the luggage check-in counter.
3. My father asked me to take this letter to the ________________.
4. She used a pair of ________________ to finish the bowl of noodles.
5. They made memories worth a ________________ on their trip.
6. The student wrote down the questions in her ________________.

Homonyms are words that have the same sound and spelling but different meanings.

Examples: I **saw** the carpenter chopping down a tree. (past tense of *see*)
He used a sharp **saw** to make his job easier. (a cutting tool with a long blade)
'It is **just** a tiny price to pay.' (only a small amount, not the whole)
They are fighting for a **just** cause. (something morally right or acceptable)

B. Make two sentences with each of these homonyms. Use the word in a different sense for each sentence.

1. land 2. chop 3. swing 4. drop 5. race 6. watch

Activity

completing a fact sheet

A fact sheet contains essential information on a topic in short, simple sentences. While reading an article or a paragraph, we often read quickly to locate the important ideas and keywords. This skill is useful while creating a fact sheet.

Read the passage on the heat wave in India in 2023 and complete the fact sheet.

A record-breaking heat wave hit India in April 2023. The states of West Bengal, Bihar, Odisha, Jharkhand and coastal Andhra Pradesh had temperatures above 44 degrees Celsius. In the north, New Delhi recorded over 40 degrees Celsius in April.

The extreme heat also had affected the wildlife in the country. In May 2023, three cheetah cubs died at the Kuno National Park due to weakness caused by the extreme heat.

A study by World Weather Attribution, a group of scientists studying climate change, found that in many parts of Asia, temperatures rose by at least 2 degrees Celsius. They said that the heat wave became 30 times more likely in India and Bangladesh because of the climate change in these countries.

1. States affected by the heat wave: ____________
2. Temperature recorded in West Bengal and Jharkhand: ____________
3. Temperature recorded in Delhi: ____________
4. Place where cheetah cubs died: ____________
5. Cause of cheetah cubs' death: ____________
6. Findings of World Weather Attribution: ____________

Explore More

Read the poem 'Daffodils' by William Wordsworth about the poet's delight when he sees many daffodils beside a lake.

Watch the short documentary *The Man of the Trees* by Andrea Trivero about a man from Burkina Faso in West Africa who works tirelessly to take care of trees.

Project 1

bagless day activity

SUSTAINABLE DEVELOPMENT GOALS 4 QUALITY EDUCATION

A. In the chapter 'Children of India', you read about the challenges children face while going to school. With your teacher's help, arrange a class visit to a school nearby. Observe the facilities provided and interact with the students. Then, in groups of four, discuss the following points about the visit and present them in class.

21ST CENTURY Initiative

- how their classrooms and playground are different from yours
- the number of students in each class
- facilities which you found similar to your school's
- something you noticed in the school which you wish you had in your school
- something you would like to change in the school you visited

After the activity, grade the performance of your group members on a scale of 1–10 based on the criteria in the table.

Group members	Observation skills	Participation in discussion	Fluency in speaking	Impact and confidence	Total

SUSTAINABLE DEVELOPMENT GOALS 4 QUALITY EDUCATION

B. In the chapter 'How I Taught My Grandmother to Read', you read about the grandmother who decides to learn to read and write. Now, design a brochure for a campaign in your school, titled 'Each One Teach One'.

21ST CENTURY Creativity

'Each One Teach One' is a concept that tells us to help people who do not have access to education by teaching them how to read. The campaign's objective is to encourage students to take out some time to teach.

You can include the following elements in your brochure:

- First fold: a slogan and an image related to the theme 'Each One Teach One'
- Second fold: importance of knowing how to read and write. You can write about:
  a. why reading and writing is useful
  b. why we should promote it
- Third fold: list the various ways one can implement 'Each One Teach One'
  a. teaching older people you know who could not receive education
  b. teaching needy children in your neighbourhood
  c. teaching at local orphanages

Making a brochure

- Turn a blank A4 sheet of paper paper sideways so that the longer side is up.
- Use a pencil and a ruler to divide the page into three parts.
- Fold both the left and the right side towards the centre.
- The trifold paper that you get is your brochure!
  Use each side of the folds as a panel to write on.

UNIT IV

Fantasy

Warm-up

A. Imagine that you decided to write a story set in a magical world with a fantasy creature as the main character. Fill in the details about your main character, and then draw a picture based on them.

____

(Name of the character)

Species: ______________________

Age: ______________________

Power: ______________________

Weakness: ______________________

Likes/Dislikes: ______________________

Purpose: ______________________

Other details: ______________________

____

(Draw your character here.)

B. Do you enjoy reading fantasy stories? Solve the riddles and find the names of these magical places.

1. Many flying broomsticks and magical potions all around,
   I am sure you could guess in which school they could be found! H _ _ _ A _ T _
2. A rabbit in a waistcoat,
   How exciting, is it not?
   But wait, for this story has a strange plot!
   Talking animals, tea parties, and funny tales to be told,
   All because a little girl goes down a rabbit hole! W _ N _ _ R L _ _ D

3. A place with people no more than six inches tall,
   Is visited by a stranger when his ship has a 'fall',
   Soon he is tied down with many ropes bound,
   To him they are like tiny threads, for he's a giant to those around! L _ _ _ I _ _ T
4. Read carefully, for this one is a bit tough,
   A girl with her little dog whisked away by a tornado, how rough!
   Fear not, for soon three strange friends they shall make,
   And set upon a journey to find a wizard for their sake! L _ _ D OF _ Z

fantasy

7

Turkish Delight

C. S. Lewis

Curricular Goals

- develop a comprehensive range of vocabulary in different contexts
- recognize basic linguistic aspects and use them in expression
- communicate effectively using language skills for analysis and response
- write about thoughts, feelings, and experiences of social events

Competencies

- can use words contextually and words related to taste
- can understand direct and indirect speech
- can recognize stressed and unstressed syllables
- can craft persuasive arguments and write a story based on a picture

Reading

a *In the middle of World War II, siblings Peter, Susan, Edmund and Lucy Pevensie are sent away from London to live with a professor in the English countryside. While exploring the large house in which the professor lives, Lucy, the youngest child, discovers the magical world of Narnia upon accidentally entering a wardrobe and meets many characters there, including a faun called Mr Tumnus. Her older siblings don't believe her, but one day, Edmund secretly follows Lucy into the wardrobe and finds himself in Narnia too. While looking for her, he meets a mysterious woman on a* ***sledge*** *driven by a dwarf. She calls herself the Queen of Narnia. Read on to find out what happens next.*

But what are you?' said the Queen again. 'Are you an overgrown dwarf that has cut off its beard?'

'No, **Your Majesty,**' said Edmund, 'I'm a boy.'

'A boy!' said she. 'Do you mean you are a Son of Adam?' Edmund stood still, saying nothing. He was too confused by this time to understand what the question meant. '

Answer me,' said the Queen, 'or I shall lose my patience. Are you human?'

'Yes, Your Majesty,' said Edmund.

'And how, **pray**, did you come to enter my **dominions**?'

'Please, Your Majesty, I came in through a wardrobe.'

'A wardrobe? What do you mean?'

'I opened a door and just found myself here, Your Majesty,' said Edmund.

Cross-curricular Corner

In Christianity, Adam and Eve are believed to be the first man and woman. The Queen refers to Edmund as a 'Son of Adam' because he is a human being, as opposed to the magical creatures in Narnia.

How did Edmund enter Narnia?

sledge: vehicle for travelling over snow and ice, with long narrow pieces of wood or metal instead of wheels

your majesty: a title of respect used to address a king or a queen

pray: used to mean 'please' when you are asking a question or telling somebody to do something

dominions: areas of land that are governed and controlled by someone

'Ha!' said the Queen, speaking to herself. 'A door. A door from the world of men! I have heard of such things. This may wreck all. But he is only one, and he is easily dealt with.'

She rose from her seat and looked Edmund full in the face, her eyes flaming and raised her wand. Edmund felt sure that she was going to do something dreadful, but he seemed unable to move. Then, she appeared to change her mind.

'My poor child,' she said in quite a different voice, 'how cold you look! Come and sit with me here on the sledge.'

Edmund dared not disobey; he stepped on to the sledge and sat at her feet, and she put a fold of her fur **mantle** around him and **tucked** it **in**.

'Perhaps something hot to drink?' said the Queen.

'Yes, please, Your Majesty,' said Edmund, whose teeth were chattering.

The Queen took out a very small bottle which looked as if it were made of copper. Holding out her arm, she let one drop fall from it on the snow. The moment it touched the snow there was a hissing sound, and there stood a jewelled cup full of something that steamed. The dwarf handed it to Edmund with a bow and not a very nice smile. Edmund felt much better as he began to sip the hot drink. It was sweet and foamy and creamy, and it warmed him right down to his toes.

Cross-curricular Corner

Turkish Delight or 'Lokum' is a jelly candy with chopped pistachios inside. It is coated with powdered sugar on the outside. It is known to have been produced in Turkey and Iran (Persia) since the late 18th century.

'What would you like best to eat?' said the Queen **presently**.

'Turkish Delight, please, Your Majesty,' said Edmund.

The Queen let another drop fall from her bottle on the snow, and instantly there appeared a round box, tied with green silk ribbon, which turned out to contain several **pounds** of the best Turkish Delight. Each piece was sweet and light to the very centre. Edmund had never tasted anything more delicious.

mantle: a piece of clothing without sleeves worn over other clothes in the past

tucked in: (here) covered someone and made them comfortable

presently: immediately

pounds: a unit of weight; one pound is equal to 0.454 kilograms

While he was eating, the Queen kept asking him questions. At first, Edmund tried to remember that it is rude to speak with one's mouth full, but soon he thought only of trying to shovel down[1] as much Turkish Delight as he could. The more he ate, the more he wanted to eat, and he never asked himself why the Queen should be so **inquisitive**. She got him to tell her that he had one brother and two sisters, that one of his sisters had already been in Narnia and had met a **faun** there, and that no one except them knew anything about Narnia. 'You are sure there are just four of you,' she asked, 'neither more nor less?'

Edmund, with his mouth full of Turkish Delight, kept on saying, 'Yes, I told you that before,' and forgetting to call her 'Your Majesty' but she did not seem to mind now.

At last, the Turkish Delight was finished, and Edmund was wishing that she would ask him whether he would like some more. For this was **enchanted** Turkish Delight and anyone who had once tasted it would want more and more of it. But she did not offer him anymore. Instead, she said to him, 'Son of Adam, I should so much like to see your brother and sisters. Will you bring them to me?'

'I'll try,' said Edmund, looking at the empty box.

'Because, if you did come again – bringing them with you, of course – I would be able to give you more Turkish Delight. I cannot do it now; the magic will only work once. In my own house, it would be another matter.'

Common idioms and phrases

1. **shovel something down:** This idiom means to put large quantities of food into one's mouth very quickly.

'Why can't we go to your house now?' said Edmund. When he had first got on to the sledge, he had been afraid that she might drive away with him to some unknown place from which he would not be able to get back, but he had forgotten about that fear now.

'It is a lovely place, my house,' said the Queen. 'There are whole rooms full of Turkish Delight. I have no children of my own. I want a nice boy whom I could bring up as a prince and who would be King of Narnia when I am gone. He would wear a gold crown and eat Turkish Delight all day long; and you are much the cleverest and handsomest young man I've ever met. I think I would like to make you the prince someday, when you bring the others to visit me.'

'Why not now?' said Edmund.

'Oh, but if I took you there now,' said she, 'I shouldn't see your brother and your sisters. You are to be the King. You must have **courtiers** and **nobles**. I will make your brother a **Duke** and your sisters **Duchesses**.'

Why could the Queen not give Edmund more Turkish Delight?

inquisitive: eager to know or learn about something

faun: an imaginary creature who looks like a man with goat ears, horns, tail and legs

enchanted: under a spell

courtiers: attendants at a royal court

nobles: people who come from a family of high social rank

duke, duchesses: a nobleman and noblewomen of the highest rank, below the prince and princess

'There's nothing special about them,' said Edmund, 'and anyway, I could always bring them some other time.'

'Ah, but once you were in my house,' said the Queen, 'you would be enjoying yourself so much that you wouldn't want the bother of going to fetch them. No. You must go back to your own country and come to me another day, *with them*, you understand?'

'But I don't even know the way back to my own country,' **pleaded** Edmund.

'That's easy,' answered the Queen. 'Do you see that lamp?' She pointed with her wand and Edmund turned and saw the same lamp post under which Lucy had met the faun. 'Beyond that is the way to the world of men. Now, look the other way and tell me if you can see two little hills rising above the trees.'

'I think I can,' said Edmund.

'My house is between those two hills. So, the next time you come, you have only to find the lamp post and look for those two hills and walk through the woods till you reach my house. I might have to be very angry with you if you came alone.'

Where is the Queen's house?

'I'll do my best,' said Edmund.

'And you need not tell them about me,' said the Queen. 'It would be fun to keep it a secret between us two, wouldn't it? Make it a surprise for them. A clever boy like you will easily think of some excuse. If your sister has met one of the fauns, she may have heard strange stories about me – nasty stories that might make her afraid to come to me.'

While she spoke, she signalled to the dwarf to drive on, and as the sledge swept away, the Queen waved to Edmund, calling out, 'Next time! Don't forget. Come soon.'

Edmund was still staring after the sledge when he heard someone calling his name. Lucy was coming towards him from another part of the woods.

'Oh, Edmund!' she cried. 'So, you've got in too! Isn't it wonderful, – '

'All right,' said Edmund, 'you were right, and it is a magic wardrobe after all. I'll say I'm sorry if you like. But where on earth have you been? I've been looking for you everywhere.'

pleaded: asked for something in a very strong and serious way

'If I had known you had got in, I would have waited for you,' said Lucy who was too excited to notice how **snappishly** Edmund spoke or how **flushed** and strange his face was.

'I've been having lunch with dear Mr Tumnus, the faun, and the White Witch has done nothing to him for letting me go, so he thinks she can't have found out and perhaps everything is going to be all right after all.'

'The White Witch?' said Edmund, 'who's she?'

'She is a terrible person,' said Lucy. 'She calls herself the Queen of Narnia, though she has no right to be queen at all, and all the fauns and **dryads** and **naiads** and dwarfs and animals – at least all the good ones – hate her. She can turn people into stone, and she has made a magic so that it is always winter in Narnia – but it never gets to Christmas. She drives about on a sledge, drawn by a reindeer, with her wand in her hand and a crown on her head.'

Edmund was already feeling uncomfortable from having eaten too many sweets, and when he heard that the lady he had made friends with was a dangerous witch, he felt even more uncomfortable. But he wanted to taste that Turkish Delight more than anything else.

'Let's go home,' he said.

'Yes, let's,' said Lucy. 'I am glad you've got in too. The others will have to believe in Narnia now that both of us have been there. What fun it will be.'

But Edmund secretly thought that it would not be as good fun for him. He would have to admit that Lucy had been right in front of all the others, and he felt sure the others would all be on the side of the fauns and the animals; but he was already more than half on the side of the witch.

By this time, they had walked a good way. Then suddenly, they felt coats around them instead of branches, and the next moment they were both standing outside the wardrobe in the empty room.

What did Edmund secretly think?

'Come on then,' said Lucy, 'let's find the others. What a lot we shall have to tell them! And what wonderful adventures we shall have now that we're all in it together.'

snappishly: in an angry, impatient way
flushed: (of a person) with a red face
dryads, naiads: mythological nature spirits who live in the woods and waterbodies

In a Nutshell

Who Edmund, the White Witch, Lucy

Where Narnia, a magical kingdom

What The White Witch tempted Edmund into telling her about his siblings.

How She fed him enchanted Turkish delight.

About the author

C. S. Lewis (1898–1963) was a British scholar and novelist. He taught English literature at the Universities of Oxford and Cambridge. He is best known for his fantasy series *The Chronicles of Narnia*.

Comprehension HOTS

A. Answer the questions in a few lines.

1. What creature did the Queen think Edmund was at first? Why?
2. Why do you think the Queen's behaviour changed suddenly? What did she offer Edmund?
3. What did Lucy tell Edmund about the White Witch? Do you think she was right?

B. Complete the character studies of these people in the story. Then, use the information to write short paragraphs on them.

Character	Qualities	Lines from the passage
Edmund	1. *greedy* 2. 3.	
the Queen	1. 2. 3.	1. *... you needn't tell them about me.*
Lucy	1. 2. 3.	

ia **C. Answer the questions as directed.**

1. The Queen and the White Witch are different people. Write 'true' or 'false'. ________
2. Edmund did not question why the Queen was so inquisitive because
   a. he trusted the queen.
   b. the enchanted Turkish Delight dulled his common sense.
   c. she told him that she would make him the King.
3. Why did the Queen want their meeting to be a secret?
   a. She wanted it to be a surprise for Edmund's siblings.
   b. She had ill intentions towards the children.
   c. She was scared of Lucy telling Edmund about the Queen's wrongdoings.
4. Edmund secretly thought it wouldn't be fun if their other siblings found out that he had been to Narnia too because he wanted to eat all the Turkish Delight himself. Write 'true' or 'false'. Correct the statement if it is false. ____________________
   ____

Life Skills and Values

trust, resisting temptation

21ST CENTURY Critical Thinking

1. Edmund agreed with whatever the Queen said, not questioning her intentions even though he had just met her. Do you think one should trust strangers?
2. Edmund felt uncomfortable when he realisd that he had made friends with a dangerous witch. Why was he still more than half on her side?
3. Do you think Edmund was right to give in to the Witch's temptation? What would you have done in his place?

Vocabulary

contextual usage: crossword

A. Complete the crossword with words from the story.

Across

5. turn red or orange in colour
6. a nature spirit who lives in the woods
7. feminine form of *duke*
8. producing a mass of small bubbles

Down

1. a mythical creature with goat legs
2. ask for something in a strong and emotional way
3. good-looking
4. completely destroy something

words related to taste

This story uses several words related to taste.

Examples: Edmund felt much better as he began to sip the hot drink. It was **foamy**, **sweet** and **creamy**.

B. Fill in the blanks with the given words related to taste.

tangy   milky   hot   bland   bitter   sharp

1. The chilli sauce we bought last week is very ________.
2. Arun likes the ________, salty flavour of blue cheese.
3. 'Brinjal cooked with neem leaves may be ________ but it tastes heavenly,' my grandfather exclaimed.
4. The first time Thiru had *chaat*, he was amazed at the burst of ________, sweet and spicy flavours.
5. Susie dislikes having porridge. She says it tastes ________.
6. The Belgian chocolates that my brother gifted me were very smooth and ________.

Grammar

Read these sentences.

Edmund said to the Queen, 'I opened a door and found myself here.'
Edmund told the Queen that he had opened a door and found himself there.

The first sentence is in **direct speech** as the exact words of the speaker are quoted.

The second sentence is in **indirect speech** as the words of the speaker are reported, and not directly quoted.

In indirect speech, we do not use quotation marks, but use reporting verbs such as *said*, *asked*, *exclaimed*, *suggested* and *requested*, followed by the word that to report the words of the speaker.

Look at this chart for the changes we make while converting direct speech to indirect speech.

Direct speech → Indirect speech

- **person**: the first person *(I, we)* → the third person *(he, she, they)*
- **pronoun**: *this* → *that*; *these* → *those*
- **time/place words**: *now* → *then*; *today* → *that day*; *tomorrow* → *the next day/the following day*; *here* → *there*
- **tense**: simple present tense → simple past tense; simple past tense → past perfect tense

ia Rewrite these sentences in indirect speech.

1. Mridula said, 'I want to have some ice cream.'
2. Ritu said to Rohini, 'We can study at my house tomorrow.'
3. I said to my brother, 'You need to start exercising regularly.'
4. The teacher said to the students, 'Lunch break starts at noon.'
5. Sana said, 'It is a beautiful day today.'
6. Joanna said, 'The drongo is darker than the crow.'
7. Salim said, 'I miss my grandparents every day.'

Study Skills

Pronunciation

stressed and unstressed syllables

A syllable is a part of a word with a single vowel sound. A word can have one or many syllables.

Examples: **good**, **flushed** (one syllable)
admit (ad + mit), **standing** (stand + ing) (two syllables)

In words which have two syllables, the syllable that is said with more stress or force is the **stressed syllable**. The **unstressed syllable** is that part of the word which has no stress.

Say these words aloud.

Turkish (Turk + ish)   per**haps** (per + haps)

Notice that the syllables in bold are said with more stress. So, *Turk* and *haps* are the stressed syllables, whereas *ish* and *per* are the unstressed syllables in these words.

Listen to these words. Then, divide them into syllables and identify the stressed and unstressed syllables.

1. sandwich
2. exhaust
3. purple
4. disturb
5. teacher
6. refill
7. mistake
8. selfish
9. basin

Listening

listening for information

Listen to an imaginary conversation among the Pevensie children and answer the questions.

1. What did Edmund say that they always wanted to try?
2. What did Lucy have at Mr Tumnus' house?
3. What is the name of the book that Edmund found in the library?
4. Which special ingredient was mentioned in the recipe?
5. What did Susan fear that her two siblings were planning?

Speaking

conversation: making plans

Collaboration Communication

Imagine that you have discovered a portal to a secret world with your friends, and you plan to spend a few days there during your vacation. Work in pairs and enact a conversation about preparing a list of things you will need and whether or not you should inform your parents about it.

You can talk about the following:

- the food items that you will carry with you
- the place where you will live
- the tools you will need
- activities that you will do there
- means through which you'd protect yourself

Useful words and phrases

- I cannot believe we found...
- Let us pack...
- We might need...
- Should we tell...
- If we tell them, they would...

Writing

picture composition

Creativity

Look at the picture and write a story based on it. While planning your story, think of the setting, the characters, the main events of the plot and what happens in the end. Fill in the details in the given mind map. Then, write the story.

setting:
where:

when:

↓

major characters:

minor characters

↓

plot/problem:

↓ ↓ ↓

event 1:	event 2:	event 3:

↓ ↓ ↓

outcome:

Explore More

Read the book *The Lion, The Witch and The Wardrobe*, the first in *The Chronicles of Narnia* series by C. S. Lewis, from which this extract was taken. Find out what happens to the Pevensie siblings.

Watch the animated film *Spirited Away* by Hayao Miyazaki about 10-year-old Chihiro who rescues her parents from an empty magical amusement park.

Listen to the song 'This Wandering Day' by Bear McCreary, from the TV series, *The Lord of the Rings: The Rings of Power*. The song celebrates the spirit of adventure and curiosity about the world.

8 Lord of Tartary

Walter de la Mare

Curricular Goals

- explore the structure of literary devices in poetry
- communicate effectively using language skills for description and analysis

→

Competencies

- can recognize rhyming words
- can identify repetition in a poem
- can make a poster

Reading

a *Have you ever dreamt of ruling over a mighty kingdom? What would you wish for in such a life? Read this poem about the speaker's wish to be the lord of an imaginary land and his dreams of the rich life he would lead there.*

If I were Lord of Tartary,
Myself, and me alone,
My bed should be of ivory,
Of beaten gold my throne;
And in my court should peacocks **flaunt**,
And in my forests tigers **haunt**,
And in my pools great fishes **slant**
Their fins athwart the sun.

If I were Lord of Tartary,
Trumpeters every day
To all my meals should **summon** me,
And in my courtyards **bray**;
And in the evening lamps should shine,
Yellow as honey, red as wine,
While harp, and flute, and **mandolin**
Made music[1] sweet and gay.

Literary term

1. This is an example of **alliteration**. The words *mandolin*, *made* and *music* have the same /m/ sound.

Cross-curricular Corner

Tartary or Tatary was a term used in Western European literature to refer to Central Asia and its bordering areas at a time when Europeans knew nothing about the region.

flaunt: show off
haunt: visit or appear in a place repeatedly
slant their fins athwart the sun: turn their fins so that sunlight would pass through them
summon: call
bray: make a loud and harsh sound
mandolin: a musical instrument that looks like a small guitar with four pairs of strings

If I were Lord of Tartary,
I'd wear a robe of beads,
White, and gold, and green they'd be –
And small and thick as seeds;
And **ere** should **wane** the **morning star**,
I'd **don** my robe and **scimitar**.
And zebras seven should draw my car
Through Tartary's dark **glades**.

Lord of the fruits of Tartary.
Her rivers silver-pale!
Lord of the hills of Tartary.
Glen, **thicket**, wood, and **dale**!
Her flashing stars, her scented breeze,
Her trembling lakes, like foamless seas,
Her bird-delighting **citron-trees**,
In every purple **vale**!

What would the poet wear if he were Lord of Tartary?

ere: before
wane: decrease in brightness
don: wear
morning star: the sun
scimitar: a type of sword with a curved blade
glades: small open spaces in forests
thicket: bushes growing closely together
dale: an open valley
citron-trees: trees with citrus fruits
glen, vale: valley

In a Nutshell

Who the speaker, who could be a young boy

What He wishes to rule over the imaginary land of Tartary, which is filled with riches and natural beauty.

About the poet

Walter de la Mare (1873–1956) was an English poet and novelist. He is best known for his works for children. His notable works include *Bells and Grass*, *Collected Stories for Children* and *O Lovely England*.

Understanding the Poem

HOTS

ia **A. Choose the correct answers.**

1. In the poem, the speaker uses his ____________ to describe Tartary.
   a. memory b. imagination c. hard work
2. Stanza 1 discusses ______________________________.
   a. how much the speaker loves animals
   b. the furniture and the animals that the speaker wants
   c. the speaker's love for riches

3. Stanza 3 discusses ______________________.
    a. the animals the speaker would have in his courtyard
    b. the things the speaker would tell his courtiers
    c. how the speaker would dress and travel through Tartary

4. Stanza 4 discusses ______________________.
    a. the natural beauty of Tartary
    b. the trees the speaker wants to grow in Tartary
    c. what a wealthy land Tartary is

B. Answer these questions in a few lines.

1. The speaker says that if he were the Lord of Tartary, his mealtimes would be very special occasions. Note down the lines in the poem which say so.
2. The poem uses similes to describe the lamps that would shine in the evening. Identify and explain them.
3. Explain these lines in your own words.
    a. *And ere should wane the morning star, / I'd don my robe and scimitar.*
    b. *bird-delighting citron-trees*
4. Look at the two given word pairs. They are related to each other based on a common logic. Understand it and complete the second word pair.
   tiger: wild :: cow: ______________
5. Describe the robe the speaker wants to wear.
6. What are some of the elements of nature that the poet describes in the last stanza? Write down the adjectives he uses to describe them.

Life Skills and Values

imagination

21ST CENTURY Critical Thinking

1. The poem is about a young child wishing to rule a beautiful, imaginary land. Do you ever imagine being somewhere else? What kind of a place would it be and what features would it have?
2. Do you think imagination helps us to think of what we want to be when we are older? What do you dream of being when you grow up? Discuss in class.

Vocabulary

rhyming words

Read these lines.

And in my court should peacocks **flaunt**,
And in my forests tigers **haunt**

In this pair of sentences, the ending words *flaunt* and *haunt* rhyme.

Words that have the same ending sound are called **rhyming words**.

ia **A. Identify three other pairs of lines in the poem which rhyme and underline the rhyming words.**

repetition

Repetition is a literary device where the same word, phrase or a sentence is repeated at intervals to emphasize a particular idea and to create rhythm.

Example: The line **If I were the Lord of Tartary** has been repeated in the poem.

ia **B. Read these verses and underline the instances of repetition.**

1. It was many and many years ago,
   In a kingdom by the sea,
   That a maiden there lived whom you may know …
   I was a child and she was a child,
   In this kingdom by the sea …

2. Speak gently, Spring, and make no sudden sound;
   for in my windy valley, yesterday, I found
   New-born foxes squirming on the ground –
   speak gently.

3. The woods are lovely, dark, and deep,
   But I have promises to keep
   And miles before I go to sleep,
   And miles before I go to sleep.

Activity

making a poster

ART INTEGRATION · 21ST CENTURY Creativity

Imagine that you have been appointed as the travel guide to the land of Tartary. Design a poster to invite tourists to visit Tartary.

Remember the following points:

- Mention the tourist spots in Tartary and the best time to visit.
- Include names of relevant websites with information on Tartary.
- Use a catchy slogan like, 'Experience Wonder, Tour Tartary Today!'
- Add pictures to make your poster attractive.

Explore More

Read the book *Alice in Wonderland* by Lewis Carroll about a young girl, Alice, who has many adventures after she falls into a rabbit hole and ends up in Wonderland, a magical world.

Watch the 2022 Disney film *Strange World* directed by Don Hall about a family of explorers who journey to a mysterious land to save a miracle plant.

Listen to the song 'If I Were King of the Forest' sung by Judy Garland in the 1939 film *The Wizard of Oz*. It is about the Cowardly Lion, a character in the story, and his desire to rule the forest.

UNIT V

Encounters with the Wild

Warm-up

A. The United Nations Sustainable Development goal 15 aims to prevent biodiversity loss. While scorpions might come across as dangerous creatures, they play a vital role in the ecosystem. Fill in the blanks using words from the box and discover interesting facts about scorpions.

night	glow	ten years	underwater	ride	courtship	2000

1. Baby scorpions ______________ on their mother's back till their shells become hard.
2. A wild scorpion lives up to ______________.
3. Scorpions usually have a long ______________ dance.
4. Scorpions ______________ under ultraviolet light.
5. There are around ______________ scorpion species.
6. Scorpions usually hunt at ______________.
7. Scorpions can survive ______________ for about 48 hours.

B. Do you know what these endangered animals are hunted for? Work in pairs and answer. The words in the box will help you.

horn	fur
shell	meat
skin	tusks

1. Amur leopard ______________

4. Hawksbill sea turtle ______________

2. African rhinoceros ______________

5. Cross River gorilla ______________

3. Sumatran elephant ______________

6. Chinese alligator ______________

adventure 9

An Unexpected Guest

Gerald Durrell

Curricular Goals

- recognize basic linguistic aspects like types of verbs, use of idioms, similes and adverbs
- listens critically and raises probing questions about social experiences
- identify main points and summarize from a careful reading of the text

Competencies

- can understand and use similes
- can identify transitive and intransitive verbs, and use adverbs correctly
- can express opinions on a topic, and sequence events in a story to summarize

Reading

a *Have you ever looked at a garden wall and found a completely different world there? Read this story of a young boy and his adventures with the creatures who live on such a wall.*

Who were the shyest of the wall creatures?

The crumbling wall that surrounded the sunken garden alongside the house was a rich hunting ground for me. The shyest of the wall creatures were the most dangerous; you hardly ever saw one unless you looked for it, and yet there must have been several hundred living in the cracks of the wall. Slide a knife-blade carefully under a piece of the loose plaster and move it gently away from the brick, and there, **crouching** beneath it, would be a little black scorpion an inch long, looking as though he were made out of polished chocolate.

They were weird-looking things, with their flattened, oval bodies, their neat, crooked legs, the enormous crab-like claws, **bulbous** and neatly jointed as **armour**, and the tail like a string of brown beads ending in a **sting** like a rose thorn. The scorpion would lie there quietly as you examined him, only raising his tail in an almost apologetic sign of warning if you breathed too hard on him. If you kept him in the sun too long, he would simply turn his back on you and walk away under another section of plaster.

crouching: keeping body close to the ground by bending legs
bulbous: shaped liked a bulb
armour: special metal clothing that soldiers wore in the past to protect their bodies while fighting
sting: the sharp pointed part of an insect or creature that can pierce the skin, leaving a painful and poisonous wound

I grew very fond of these scorpions. I found them to be pleasant, quiet creatures with the most charming habits. Provided you did nothing silly or clumsy (like putting your hand on one), they treated you with respect, their one desire being to get away and hide as quickly as possible.

By crouching under the wall at night with a torch, I managed to catch some brief glimpses of their wonderful **courtship** dances. They stood and **waltzed** slowly in circles among the moss cushions, claw in claw.

The family had not allowed scorpions in the house. Then one day I found a fat female scorpion in the wall, wearing what at first glance appeared to be a pale **fawn** fur coat. Looking closely, I saw that this strange garment was made up of a mass of tiny babies clinging to the mother's back. I was delighted by this family, and made up my mind to smuggle them to my bedroom so that I might keep them and watch them grow up. With great care, I placed the mother and her family into a matchbox, and hurried to the villa.

It was rather unfortunate that just as I entered the door, lunch should be served. I placed the matchbox carefully on the **mantelpiece** in the drawing room, so that the scorpions could get plenty of air, and made my way to the dining room and joined the family for the meal. **Dawdling** over my food, quietly feeding Roger under the table and listening to the family arguing, I completely forgot about my exciting new captures. At one point, Larry, having finished eating, walked to the mantelpiece and picked up the matchbox. Without any idea of my **impending doom** I watched him interestedly as, still talking, he opened the matchbox.

Now, I maintain to this day that the female scorpion meant no harm. She was nervous and a little annoyed at being shut up in a matchbox for so long, and so she took the first opportunity to escape. She got out of the box with great rapidity, her babies clinging on desperately, and **scuttled** on to the back of Larry's hand. There, not quite certain what to do next, she paused, her sting curved up at the ready. Larry, feeling the movement of her claws, glanced down to see what it was, and from that moment on, things got very confusing.

He uttered a roar of fright that made Lugaretzia drop a plate and brought Roger out from beneath the table, barking wildly. With a flick of his hand, he sent the unfortunate scorpion flying down the table. She landed midway between Margo and Leslie, scattering babies like **confetti** as she thumped on the cloth. Thoroughly enraged at this treatment, the creature **sped** towards Leslie, her sting quivering. Leslie leapt to his feet, overturning his chair, and flicked out desperately with his napkin, sending the scorpion rolling across the cloth towards Margo, who let out a scream that any railway engine would have been proud to produce. Mother, surprised by this sudden change from peace to utter confusion, put on her glasses and looked down the table to see what was the cause.

At that moment, Margo, in a vain attempt to stop the scorpion, hurled a glass of water at it.

The shower missed the animal completely, but successfully soaked Mother, who, not being able to stand cold water, lost her breath and sat **gasping** at the end of the table, unable even to **protest**.

What was Margo's scream compared to?

courtship: the special way animals behave to attract mates
waltzed: danced
fawn: light yellow-brown colour
mantelpiece: a shelf above a fireplace
dawdling: taking a long time
impending doom: an unavoidable, terrible thing that is about to happen
scuttled: ran with quick short steps
confetti: small pieces of coloured paper that people throw at weddings and other special events
sped: moved along quickly
gasping: taking quick deep breaths with the mouth open, due to surprise or pain
protest: to disagree or show objection

The scorpion had now gone to ground[1] under Leslie's plate, while her babies **swarmed** wildly all over the table. Roger, also puzzled by the panic, but determined to do his share, ran round and round the room, barking wildly.

'Look out! Look out! They're coming!' screamed Margo.

'All we need is a book,' roared Leslie; 'don't panic, hit 'em with a book.'

'What on earth's the *matter* with you all?' Mother kept asking, **mopping** her glasses.

'It's that boy ... he'll kill the lot of us ... Look at the table... knee-deep in scorpions ...'

'Stop screeching and get a book, for God's sake ... *Shut up*, Roger ...'

'By the grace of God I wasn't bitten ...'

'Look out ... there's another one ... Quick, quick ...'

'But *how* did the scorpions get on the table, dear?'

'That boy ... Every matchbox in the house is a death trap ...'

'Look out, it's coming towards me ... Quick, quick, do something ...'

'Hit it with your knife ... *your knife* ... Go on, hit it ...'

Common idioms and proverbs

1. **go to ground:** This idiom means to hide, especially to escape somebody who is chasing them.

Since no one had bothered to explain things to him, Roger was under the mistaken impression that the family was being attacked, and that it was his duty to defend them.

As Lugaretzia was the only stranger in the room, he came to the conclusion that she must be the responsible party, so he bit her in the ankle. This did not help matters much.

Whom did Roger bite?

By the time order returned, all the baby scorpions had hidden themselves under various plates and bits of cutlery. After many pleas on my part, backed up by Mother, Leslie's suggestion that the whole lot be **slaughtered** was rejected. While the family, still shaking, went to the drawing room, I spent half an hour rounding up the babies, picking them up in a teaspoon, and returning them to their mother's back. Then I carried them outside on a saucer and, very unwillingly released them on the garden wall.

swarmed: moved together
mopping: wiping
slaughtered: killed

The results of this incident were many. Larry developed a **phobia** about matchboxes and opened them with great caution, a handkerchief wrapped around his hand. Lugaretzia limped around the house, her ankle covered in yards of bandage for weeks after the bite had healed, and every morning, showed us how the **scabs** were doing.

But from my point of view, the worst fallout of the whole affair was that Mother decided I was running wild again, and that it was high time I received a little more education.

phobia: strong unreasonable fear

scabs: hard dry coverings that form over wounds as they heal

Why did Lugaretzia limp around the house?

In a Nutshell

Who the author and his family

What scorpions all over the lunch table

Why The scorpion and her babies escaped from a matchbox in which the author had kept them.

Where at the author's house

About the author

Gerald Durrell (1925–1995) was a British naturalist, author and zookeeper. Durrell's interest in animals grew after moving to Corfu in Greece with his family as a child. He started to collect local creatures as pets. Some of his famous works are *My Family and Other Animals* and *The Garden of Gods.*

Comprehension

HOTS

A. Complete the sentences with reference to the story.

1. The author's curiosity about the scorpions tells us that he was ____________________.
2. `Enormous crab-like claws, bulbous and neatly jointed as armour, and the tail like a string of brown beads ending in a sting' is a description of the scorpion's ____________________. (behaviour/physical appearance)
3. We know that the scorpions were mild creatures because ____________________.
4. The scorpion's pale fawn fur coat was actually ____________________.

5. The scorpion's sting is dangerous but if not disturbed, it is a ____________ creature.
6. At the end of the story, the narrator's mother concluded that the narrator was running wild again. The phrase 'running wild' here means ____________.

B. Answer the questions.

1. What behaviour of the scorpions fascinated the author? Describe their courtship dance.
2. What did the author smuggle inside a matchbox and why?
3. Why was the female scorpion annoyed? What did she do after Larry opened the matchbox?
4. Describe the scene caused by Larry, Leslie and Margo at the lunch table.
5. Why did the author's mother sit gasping at the end of the table?
6. How did Roger try to defend the family?
7. What was the worst fallout of the whole affair, according to the author?

Life Skills and Values

appreciation for wildlife

21ST CENTURY Critical Thinking

1. Do you think the author should have picked up the scorpion from the wall? Why/Why not?
2. The author's request to let the scorpions live were supported by his mother. What does this tell you about her?

Vocabulary

similes

Read this line.

She landed midway between Margo and Leslie, scattering babies **like confetti** as she thumped on the cloth.

Here, the scattering of the scorpion's babies has been compared with confetti being thrown in every direction. This is a simile.

A **simile** is a figure of speech in which someone or something is compared to a very different person or thing using *as* or *like*.

ia **Complete the similes with the suitable words.**

log midnight fiddle whistle snow cucumber

1. After clearing away a lot of clutter, my room is now as clean as a ____________.
2. The kitten Sana brought home yesterday is as white as ____________.
3. Mr Saldanha is as fit as a ____________ even though he is in his 80s.
4. He remained as cool as a ____________ and went on to win the debate.
5. It was as dark as ____________ inside the deep, lush forest.
6. After studying the whole day, I was tired and slept like a ____________.

Read these sentences.

With great care, I **placed** the mother and her family into a matchbox.

The scorpion **landed** midway between Margo and Leslie.

You have learnt that we can identify the object in a sentence by using the verb to ask the questions *who?* or *what?*

In the first sentence, the verb *placed* has the object, *the mother and her family*.

(I placed what into a matchbox? **Answer:** *the mother and her family*)

Such verbs which have an object are transitive verbs. Hence, *placed* is a transitive verb.

A **transitive verb** is a verb which needs an object to complete its meaning.

The second sentence does not have an object. The verb *landed* doesn't need an object to complete its meaning. It is intransitive.

An **intransitive verb** is one which does not need an object to complete its meaning.

Intransitive verbs can stand alone or may be followed by a phrase that gives information about the action. In the second sentence, this phrase is *midway between Margo and Leslie*.

Language Booster

Some verbs can be both transitive and intransitive depending on their usage.

Example: The cat *ate* heartily. (intransitive, as the sentence doesn't have an object)

The cat *ate* the fish. (transitive, as the sentence has an object, *fish*)

ia **A. Underline the verbs in these sentences and identify them as transitive (T) or intransitive (IT). (Hint: Find the object to identify whether the verb is transitive or intransitive.)**

1. The envelope contains important letters. ☐
2. The roller-coaster ride is thrilling. ☐
3. Geeta bought strawberries from the market. ☐
4. The cook made pasta for dinner. ☐
5. The Jan Shatabdi Express reached on time. ☐
6. The dog is sleeping on the rug. ☐

adverbs and their positions

You know that an **adverb** is a word that is used to modify or add information to a verb, an adjective or another adverb.

Look at this table which explains the various functions of adverbs.

Adverb	Position	Example
Some adverbs tell us how the action takes place.	after the verb or after the direct object of the verb	Roger ran round and round the room, barking **wildly**.
Some adverbs tell us when the action takes place.	at the end of the sentence	I will go home **now**.
Some adverbs tell us where the action takes place.	after the verb	The scorpions would lie **there**.
Some adverbs tell us how often the action takes place.	between the subject of the sentence and the verb	You **hardly** ever saw one.

ia **B. Circle the adverb in each sentence.**

1. Sushmita practised the piano regularly.
2. Rohan had always wanted to be an astronaut.
3. The nightingale sang melodiously at the break of dawn.
4. The ice cream cart is waiting here.
5. My cousins will arrive tomorrow.

ia **C. Rewrite these sentences by inserting the adverbs in the correct places.**

1. She goes to the library. (rarely)
2. I looked for my cousin. (everywhere)
3. My father leaves by 8 a.m. (always)
4. The nightingale sang. (sweetly)
5. They will announce the winners. (now)

Study Skills

Dictionary Skills

homonyms

21st Century Information Literacy

Read these words aloud, and notice how they are pronounced. These words have multiple meanings. Use your dictionary and write the correct meaning of the word based on its pronunciation.

1. live (rhymes with *dive*)
2. bow (rhymes with *row*)
3. wind (rhymes with *kind*)
4. lead (rhyming with *seed*)
5. read (rhyming with *bed*)

Listening

listening for details

Listen to a poem about different animals. Fill in the blanks with the correct words.

1. The ________________ (cat/dog) will come when called.
2. The monkey's ________________ (neck/cheek) is very bald.
3. The ________________ (parrot/goat) does not know what she says.
4. The horse will draw a ________________ (cart/chaise).
5. The squirrel likes a ________________ (nut/fruit).

Speaking

expressing an opinion

You read about the author's love for all creatures, even those whom people consider dangerous. Today, as cities expand, forests and other animal habitats are often removed. Do you think that there is a way for human beings and other living creatures to co-exist? Express your opinion in the class. You may use instances from the story to support your ideas.

Useful words and phrases

Human beings

- destroyer/protector of nature
- love for animals
- desire to domesticate

Nature

- animals survive best in their habitat
- loss of habitat forces them to move into human territories, leading to capture and loss of lives

Writing

sequencing and writing a summary

A. The following sentences describe the main events in the story. Rearrange them in the order in which the events occur.

- ☐ One day, he found a mother scorpion carrying her babies on her back on the garden wall.
- ☐ When he reached his house, lunch was going to be served, so he put the matchbox on the mantlepiece.
- ☐ When things started to settle down, the author rounded up all the scorpions, carried them outside and released them on the garden wall.
- ☐ He screamed and flicked his hand, sending the mother scorpion flying.
- ☐ The author visited the sunken garden next to the house to observe the scorpions living in a crumbling wall there.
- ☐ He decided to smuggle the scorpion family into his bedroom because he wanted to keep them and watch them grow up.
- ☐ There was a great uproar at the table, during which Margo hurled a glass of water at the author's mother and soaked her.
- ☐ The mother scorpion landed on the dining table and her babies were scattered all over it.
- ☐ Larry picked up the matchbox and opened it.

B. Now, combine all the sentences in exercise A to write the summary of the story. You may add more sentences, if necessary. Use linking words like *first, then, next* or *finally*.

Explore More

Read the book *The Story of Doctor Dolittle* by Hugh Lofting about the adventures of a doctor who can befriend animals because he speaks their language.

Watch the 2007 film *The Water Horse: Legend of the Deep* directed by Jay Russell. It is about a young boy who finds a mysterious egg while collecting seashells.

Listen to the song 'Under the Sea' by Samuel E. Wright from *The Little Mermaid*. It is about how Sebastian, the crab, prefers living underwater, away from the human world.

10 A Tiger in the Zoo

George Leslie Norris

Curricular Goals

- appreciate poems, stories and conversations and locates important ideas in them
- identify literary devices such as simile, metaphor, alliteration
- make oral presentations

Competencies

- can recognize poetic devices like imagery and onomatopoeia
- can make a presentation

Reading

a *How would you feel if someone trapped you in your room? Wouldn't you miss the playground, your friends and everything outside? Read this poem about a tiger who is trapped in a cage in the zoo and how he longs to get back to the forest.*

He **stalks** in his **vivid** stripes
The few steps of his cage,
On **pads of velvet quiet**,
In his **quiet rage**.

He should be **lurking** in shadow,
Sliding through long grass
Near the water hole
Where **plump** deer pass.

He should be **snarling** around houses
At the jungle's edge,
Baring his white **fangs**, his claws,
Terrorising the village!

But he's locked in a concrete cell,
His strength behind bars,
Stalking the length of his cage,
Ignoring visitors.

Where should the tiger be lurking?

stalks: walks in a proud and angry way
vivid: deep and bright
pads of velvet quiet: (here) soft paws of the tiger which allow him to walk quietly
quiet rage: violent anger that the tiger cannot express because he is trapped
lurking: waiting or remaining hidden to hunt
plump: full and round
fangs: long, sharp teeth of animals
terrorising: creating a state of extreme fear

He hears the last voice at night,
The **patrolling cars**,
And stares with his brilliant eyes
At the brilliant stars.

patrolling cars: cars of police or guards moving around an area to ensure there is no trouble

In a Nutshell

Who a tiger

What walking in his cage in the zoo

Why He is angry and restless because he wants to live freely in the forest.

About the poet

George Leslie Norris (1921–2006) was a Welsh poet and a short story writer. Norris was a fellow of England's Royal Academy of Literature. His notable works include *Ransoms* and *The Collected Poems*.

Understanding the Poem

HOTS

ia **A. Choose the correct options.**

1. Why do you think the tiger ignores the visitors at the zoo?
   a. He is shy and he is afraid of them.
   b. He is not interested in them because he knows they will not help him.
   c. He feels that they are boring.
2. Why does the tiger stalk in 'quiet rage'?
   a. He does not want to disturb the other animals in the zoo.
   b. He cannot express his anger the way he wants to because he is trapped.
   c. He is planning something and wants it to be a secret.
3. Which of these lines shows alliteration?
   a. 'On pads of velvet quiet'
   b. 'His strength behind bars'
   c. 'And stares with his brilliant eyes'
4. 'And stares with his brilliant eyes/ At the brilliant stars.' What do these lines tell us?
   a. They tell us about the beauty of the tiger's eyes.
   b. They tell us about the tiger's hope and longing to be free.
   c. They tell us about the tiger's boredom in his cage.
5. Which word in the poem is the opposite in meaning to 'dull'?
   a. velvet   b. brilliant   c. concrete

B. Answer the questions in a few lines.

1. How does the tiger feel in the zoo? How is his life different from the tigers in the wild?
2. According to the poem, how does the tiger terrorise the village?
3. The tiger hears the patrolling cars at night. What should he be hearing instead in his natural habitat?
4. What message does the poet convey through the poem?

Life Skills and Values

empathy, compassion, thoughtfulness

Critical Thinking · Initiative

1. The poem voices the tragedy of a tiger who is trapped in a cage in a zoo. Do you think zoos serve the purpose of protecting animals? Give reasons for your answer.
2. Imagine that you found an injured stray animal lying unattended near your house. What would you do? Share your thoughts with the class.

Vocabulary

imagery

Read these lines.

He should be lurking in shadows/Sliding through long grass …

These lines help us to picture the tiger moving freely in his natural habitat. This is an example of **visual imagery**.

ia **A. Look at the diagram that shows different kinds of imagery. Then, complete the mind map with words and phrases related to things you can see, hear, touch and taste during the monsoons.**

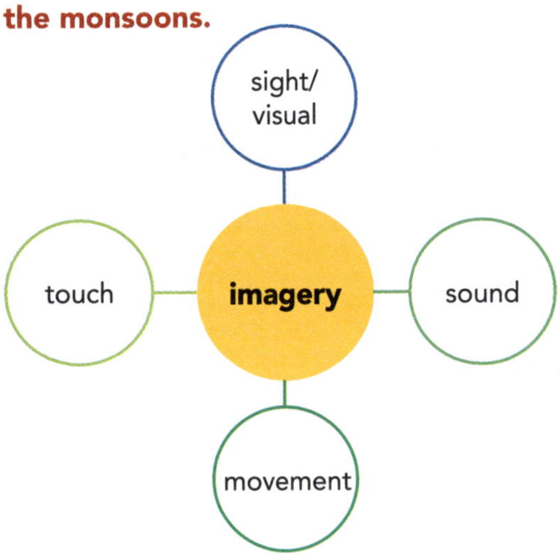

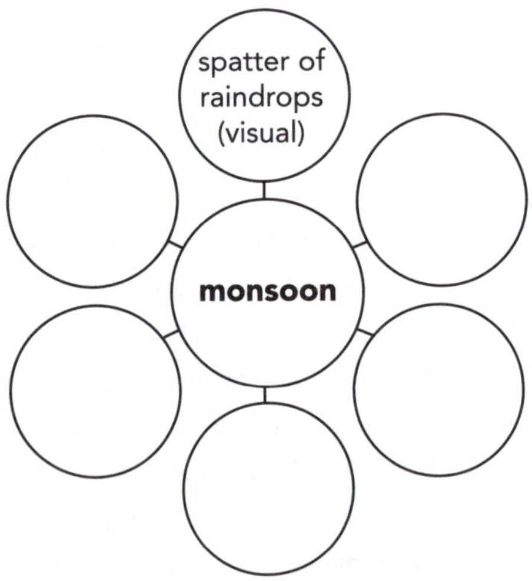

onomatopoeia

Onomatopoeia is the use of words whose pronunciation is similar to the sounds they represent.

Examples: The tiger jumped into the river with a loud **splash** and began to swim.
He should be **snarling** around houses.

ia **B. Fill in the blanks using the onomatopoeic words in the box.**

splashed	sizzled	beeps	boom	clatter

1. The *paratha* ____________ in the pan.
2. Anthony ____________ his face with cold water to wake himself up.
3. The refrigerator ____________ if the door is not closed properly.
4. The dishes fell to the floor with a ____________.
5. The loud ____________ of the fireworks scared the dog.

Activity

making a presentation

Did you know that there are 40 different species of cats on the Earth? Unfortunately, the population size of many wild cat species is decreasing. Form groups of four and choose a species of wild cat from the given list to make a presentation on. Each student should speak for two to three minutes.

Your presentation should include the following points:

- details about the animal: characteristics, habitat, food habits
- the previous and current population size; factors responsible for the loss in numbers
- organizations/programs/sanctuaries involved in raising awareness and rescue operations

List of vulnerable and endangered wild cats

- Snow leopard
- Borneo bay cat
- Andean mountain cat
- Marbled cat
- Asiatic cheetah
- Fishing cat
- Iberian lynx
- Flat-headed cat
- Clouded leopard
- Oncilla

Explore More

Read the book *Tigers Forever* by Ruskin Bond. It is collection of poems and short stories about tigers and their fight for survival against human beings.

Watch the 1942 Disney film *Bambi* about a fawn who is chosen to become the prince of the forest. As he grows up, he learns about friendship, love and protecting his dear ones.

Listen to the audio book *A Life On Our Planet*, narrated by Sir David Attenborough, about how the world has changed and his vision of the future.

UNIT
VI

Community and Neighbourhood

Warm-up

SUSTAINABLE DEVELOPMENT GOALS 11 SUSTAINABLE CITIES AND COMMUNITIES

A. The United Nations Sustainable Development goal 11 aims to make cities and communities environmentally conscious, welcoming and safe for all people. Circle the places that you feel are important to build a happy community. Then, write them in the suitable columns according to their purpose.

factory	school	hospital	stadium	housing
water tank	beauty salon	movie theatre	college	transport system
crèche	university	gym	park	recycling plant
mall/market	swimming pool	playground	office	restaurant
roads	community centre			

Education	Environment	Entertainment	Others

B. Read about the history of the palanquin or *palki* and fill in the blanks with the given words.

railways rectangular transport twentieth patterns ambulances royalty bamboo

The *palki* was a popular mode of ____________ for the rich in India. It is a ____________ wooden box, supported by poles on either end, and carried by male *palki* bearers. Palanquins were decorated with colourful designs of leaves, animals and geometric ____________. The most ornamented ones belonged to ____________ and wealthy nobles. The simplest and smallest palanquin was the *doli*, which was made of a cot or a frame supported by a ____________ pole and carried by two bearers. In British India, *dolis* were used as military ____________ to carry the injured from the battlefield. The palanquin was common till the ____________ century, after which steamers, ____________ and roads suitable for wheeled vehicles replaced it.

parable

11

A Spark Neglected Burns the House

Leo Tolstoy

Curricular Goals

- develop a comprehensive range of vocabulary in various contexts
- ability to recognize basic linguistic aspects and use them in expression
- communicate effectively using language skills for description, analysis and response
- organize thoughts and ideas to write for an intended purpose

Competencies

- can understand and use synonyms and proverbs
- can use articles, and conjunctions to express reason
- can express emotions suited to a given situation
- can write descriptions of people

Reading

a *Have you heard of the saying, 'an eye for an eye makes the whole world blind'? Read a story that narrates what happens to two men who are unwilling to forgive and forget.*

There once lived in a village a **peasant** named Ivan. He had a wife and three sons. The eldest was married, the second about to marry, and the third was a big lad who could mind the horses by himself. Ivan took care of his old father, who had been lying ill on top of the brick oven for seven years.

Cross-curricular Corner

The Russian oven is a type of brick stove usually built in the middle of a log cottage. It was used both for cooking as well as heating the room. In the severe Russian winters, it was quite common for people to sleep on top of the oven to keep warm.

Ivan had all he needed: three horses and a **colt**, a cow with a calf, and fifteen sheep. The women made all the clothing for the family, besides helping in the fields, and the men **tilled** the land. They always had enough grain to last beyond the next harvest and sold enough oats to pay the taxes and meet their other needs.

List the animals that Ivan had.

Ivan and his children might have lived on happily had it not been for a **feud** between him and his next-door neighbour, Limping Gabriel.

It all began about a **trifle**. Ivan's daughter-in-law had a hen that began laying rather early in the season, and she started collecting its eggs for Easter. One day, the hen, probably frightened by the children, flew across the fence into the neighbour's yard and laid its egg there. The woman heard the **cackling** but said to herself: 'I have no time now; I must tidy up for Sunday. I'll fetch the egg later.' In the evening, she went to the coop but found no egg. She asked her brother-in-law whether he had taken the egg. 'No,' he replied, 'your hen laid its egg in the neighbour's yard. It was there she was cackling, and she flew back across the fence from there.'

peasant: farmer
colt: young male horse
tilled: ploughed
feud: long and bitter dispute between two families or people
trifle: an unimportant matter
cackling: (of a chicken) making a loud unpleasant noise

The woman went to the neighbour's house. Gabriel's mother came out to meet her.

'What do you want, young woman?'

'Granny, my hen flew across this morning. Did she not lay an egg here?'

'We never saw anything. The Lord be thanked, our own hens started laying long ago. We have no need of other people's! And we don't go looking for eggs in other people's yards, **lass**!'

The young woman felt angry and replied in harsher tones than she should have. Soon, the women were quarrelling with each other.

'You're a thief!'

'You're starving your old father-in-law to death!'

'You're a good-for-nothing!'

'You've made a hole in the **sieve** I lent you!'

'It's our **yoke** you're carrying your pails on – you give back our yoke right now!'

They snatched off one another's shawls and began fighting. Gabriel, returning from the fields, stopped to take his mother's side. Ivan and his son too joined in. Ivan was a strong fellow. He scattered the whole lot of them and pulled a handful of hair out of Gabriel's beard. People came to see what the matter was, and the fighters were separated with difficulty.

Soon, not a day passed without a quarrel between the families. The children, too, fought with one another, having learnt to do so from their elders.

The old man, from where he lay on top of the oven, tried to **persuade** them to make peace, but they would not listen. He told them, 'It's a foolish thing, picking quarrels about such a **paltry** matter. The whole thing began with an egg. It doesn't matter who took it. Doesn't God send enough for all? If you **nurse** your anger, it will only make things worse.'

But the younger folk would not listen to him. At first the peasants only **slandered** one another; but soon, life became harder for them as they kept **suing** one another at the village assembly and before the Justice of the Peace until all the judges were tired of them.

In the seventh year, at a wedding, Ivan's son accused Gabriel of horse stealing. Gabriel was unable to control his anger and gave the man a blow that laid him up in bed for a week. Ivan immediately went to the magistrate to lodge a complaint.

lass: a young girl or a woman
sieve: a strainer
yoke: a piece of wood that is shaped to fit across a person's shoulders so that they can carry two equal loads
persuade: make somebody do something by giving them good reasons for doing it
paltry: unimportant, worthless
nurse: (here) to feel something strongly for a long time
slandered: spread lies and rumours
suing: starting legal proceedings

'How dare Gabriel hurt my son? He won't escape imprisonment, or **exile** to Siberia.'

But the son recovered soon and was up and about. The magistrate gave Gabriel a **hefty** fine, but neither imprisoned him nor sent him to Siberia. Dissatisfied, Ivan **bribed** the clerk and got Gabriel sentenced to receive twenty **lashes** with a birch rod at the district court.

When the sentence was read, Gabriel grew as pale as a sheet, turned around and went out into the passage.

What was the punishment given by the magistrate?

Ivan followed him and overheard him say, 'Very well! He will have me **flogged:** that will burn; but something of his own may burn worse than that!'

Gabriel wished to say something more but his lips **quivered**, and he turned towards the wall. Even the officials were frightened by his looks. 'He will do mischief to himself or to his neighbour,' they thought.

When Ivan reached home, he remembered how Gabriel had listened to the **sentence**, and how he had turned to the wall. His heart grew heavy. He thought how he himself would feel if he were sentenced, and he pitied Gabriel. His father, who had dragged himself with difficulty to sit with his son, shook his head when he heard of Gabriel's sentence.

'You are doing wrong, Ivan!' said he. 'It's very bad – not for him so much as for yourself! They'll flog him: but will that do you any good?'

'He'll not do it again,' said Ivan.

'What is it he'll not do again? What has he done worse than you?'

'Why, think of the harm he has done me!' said Ivan. 'He nearly killed my daughter-in-law, and now he's threatening to burn us up. Am I to thank him for it?'

The old man sighed, and said: 'Ah, lad! **Malice** blinds you. Others' sins are before your eyes, but your own are behind your back. It's not the way I used to live, lad, and it's not the way I taught you. How did his old father and I live? Why, as neighbours should! If someone upsets you, forgive him. Then life will be easy, and your heart will always be light.'

His father's words rang true to Ivan. He decided to make peace with Gabriel. But soon, everyone came home talking of the sentencing and discussing a new **row** they had had with Gabriel's household. Hearing them, Ivan's heart grew cold again. By nightfall, he had quite forgotten his father's advice.

Walking back home from his evening **chores** around the **homestead**, he heard Gabriel across the fence, muttering **hoarsely** to himself, 'He deserves his fate. What on earth is he good for?'

Ivan was **alarmed**. 'I'll just walk around the buildings to make sure everything is safe. Who can tell what he's after?' he thought.

exile: forced to live away from one's home or country
hefty: large
bribed: influenced with money or gifts
lashes: strikes or beating with a series of violent blows
flogged: whipped
quivered: trembled
sentence: (here) punishment
malice: evil intention
row: fight
chores: routine tasks
homestead: a house with lands and buildings around it
hoarsely: roughly
alarmed: worried

Stepping into the street, he reached a corner and looked along the fence. Someone quickly came out and disappeared again. Ivan stopped and stood quietly, listening and looking. Everything was still; only the leaves of the willows fluttered in the wind, and the straws of the **thatch** rustled. At first it seemed pitch dark, but when his eyes got used to the darkness, he could see the far corner, where a plough lay. Suddenly, something flared up brightly, and he saw a man **crouching**, with his back towards him, lighting a bunch of straw. In minutes, the flames were reaching up to the roof, and, standing beneath it, Gabriel was clearly visible.

Like a hawk **swooping** down on a **lark**[1], Ivan rushed at Gabriel. 'Now I'll catch him!'

At Gabriel's own gate, Ivan was about to seize him, when something struck a **stunning** blow, quite deafening him. It was Gabriel, who had picked up an oak **wedge** and hit him with it.

When Ivan came to his senses some time later, his homestead was burning. It roared and crackled like an engine at work.

Ivan tried to shout, but his breath failed him. He wanted to run, but his legs would not obey him. The flames were now leaping out of the hut. The family barely managed to save the old father. Everything else, except the horses and cattle, was lost.

What did Gabriel hit Ivan with?

Gabriel's house also caught fire. Then, the wind rising, the flames spread to the other side of the street and soon, half the village was burnt down.

The fire raged all night. When morning came, Ivan's father lay dying. Burning **embers** had fallen on him and injured him. He sent for his son.

'Ivan,' said the old man **feebly**, when he saw Ivan, 'Now, before God, say whose is the sin? What did I tell you?'

Only then did Ivan come to his senses.

'Mine, father!' he cried.

He fell on his knees, crying, 'Forgive me, father; I am guilty before you and before God. I don't know how we are to live now! What are we to do?'

Literary term

1. This is a **simile**. Ivan's rushed movement towards Gabriel is compared to the speed of a hawk's flight to catch a lark.

thatch: roof made of straw or leaves
crouching: bending or stooping
swooping: quickly flying downwards
lark: a small brown bird
stunning: making someone unconscious for a short time by hitting them on the head
wedge: chunk
embers: the burning remains of a fire
feebly: weakly

'You'll manage, Ivan,' whispered his father. 'Don't tell anyone who started the fire! Hide another man's sin, and God will forgive two of yours!' And the old man sighed, stretched out and died.

When the villagers began rebuilding, Ivan did not tell anyone what he had seen that night. Gabriel wondered why. At first he felt afraid, but after a while he got used to it. The men left off quarrelling, and then their families left off too. They lived as good neighbours should. Ivan remembered his old father's teaching: to **quench** a fire at the first spark.

Common idioms and proverbs

turn the other cheek: This idiom means to remain calm and not act in anger when somebody has hurt or angered you. It refers to what Ivan's father advised him to do.

Example: I usually *turn the other cheek* when someone is rude to me.

quench: (here) put out

In a Nutshell

Who Gabriel, Ivan and their families

What A fight between neighbours turned into a tragic incident.

How Gabriel burnt Ivan's house down.

Why Ivan got Gabriel sentenced to receive twenty lashes after the latter's blow injured Ivan's son.

About the author

Leo Tolstoy (1828–1910) was a Russian writer, considered to be one of the greatest writers of all time. He was nominated for the Nobel Prize multiple times. He wrote short stories, children's books and books for young adults, usually upholding moral or life lessons. His famous novels, *War and Peace* and *Anna Karenina* have been read and loved by people all over the world.

Comprehension

A. Answer the questions.

1. Did Ivan's family have enough for their needs? Give reasons for your answer.
2. Why did life become harder for the two families after the first row?
3. Why did Ivan go to the magistrate to lodge a complaint? Why do you think the magistrate didn't give Gabriel a harsh sentence?
4. What did Ivan see in the pitch darkness? What happened immediately after that?
5. Why didn't Ivan tell anyone what he had seen that night? What good thing happened as a result?

B. Choose the correct option.

1. Why did Ivan pity Gabriel?
   a. He remembered how he and Gabriel had been friends in the past.
   b. He felt sorry for Gabriel, as the man had made a mistake.
   c. He thought how he would feel if he were sentenced.

2. *'They will flog him, but will that do you any good?'*
   Which emotion did Ivan's father try to bring forth in his son through these words?
   a. compassion b. anger c. being sorry
3. Which word best describes Ivan's father?
   a. cunning b. wise c. jealous
4. Which of the following statements is true about Ivan?
   a. He never listened to his father's suggestions.
   b. He changed after following his father's dying advice.
   c. He complained against Gabriel to the police.
5. Ivan's father gave him advice thrice in the story. What were they?
   a. not to nurse anger, to forgive people who wrong us and to hide another person's sin
   b. God sends enough for everybody, not to do mischief to one's neighbour, forgive two sins of others
   c. not to pick quarrels over small matters, not to hurt one's neighbours, to notice one's own sins

Life Skills and Values

compassion, forgiveness

Critical Thinking

1. Explain these lines: 'Malice blinds you. Others' sins are before your eyes, but your own are behind your back.'
2. What did you learn from the story?

Vocabulary

synonyms

Words like ***quarrel*** and ***row*** have the same meaning. They are **synonyms**.

A. Choose the correct synonym for the underlined word in each sentence.

1. The farmer tilled the soil for a livelihood.
   a. watered ☐ b. ploughed ☑ c. covered ☐
2. The teacher persuaded her class to do an extra project for the second term.
   a. assured ☐ b. challenged ☐ c. convinced ☐
3. The baby's lips quivered and she broke into tears.
   a. curled ☐ b. pressed ☐ c. trembled ☐
4. One should not bear malice towards one's neighbours.
   a. hatred ☐ b. patience ☐ c. trust ☐
5. His mother was alarmed when she suddenly got a call from the school.
   a. happy ☐ b. worried ☐ c. relaxed ☐
6. The sign read 'Do not trample on the flowers'.
   a. squash ☐ b. pet ☐ c. cut ☐

proverbs

B. Match the proverbs with their meanings. Then make sentences of your own with any three of them.

Proverbs	Meanings
1. Don't judge a book by its cover.	a. Rely on one particular course of action for success.
2. Too many cooks spoil the broth.	b. Tell a secret carelessly or by mistake.
3. Look before you leap.	c. If too many people are involved in doing something, it will not be done well.
4. Let the cat out of the bag.	d. Do not form an opinion about somebody/something from their appearance only.
5. Put all your eggs in one basket.	e. Think about the possible results or dangers of something before doing it.

Grammar

articles

Articles are words that tell us whether a noun is specific or general.

The articles *a* and *an* are used before singular, general nouns.

Examples: There once lived in **a** village **an** angry peasant named Ivan.

The article *the* is used before nouns that refer to something specific.

Example: **The** hen flew into **the** neighbour's yard and laid an egg there.

A. Read this extract from 'Cousin Tribulations', a short story by Louisa May Alcott, and fill in the blanks with suitable articles.

'Happy New Year, Papa! Where is Mother?' we cried.

'_____ little boy came begging and said that his family was starving at home. Your mother went to see them.'

As Father spoke, in came Mother, looking very cold and sad.

'Not far away from here lies _____ poor woman with _____ little newborn baby. Six children are huddled into one bed to keep from freezing. _____ oldest boy came here to ask for help. My little girls, will you give them your breakfast as _____ New Year's gift?'

We sat silent for _____ minute and looked at _____ nice, hot porridge with creamy milk, and good bread and butter. 'I wish we'd eaten it up,' thought I.

'May I help carry it to _____ poor children?' asked Beth, who had _____ kindest heart.

'I can carry _____ sugar pot,' said little May, proudly giving up _____ thing she loved _____ best.

'And I shall take _____ porridge,' I burst in, ashamed of my first feeling.

'Come and help me,' said Mother, beginning to pile _____ bread and butter into _____ big basket.

Read these sentences.

Life became harder for the families. They kept suing one another at the village assembly.

Life became harder for the families **because** they kept suing one another at the village assembly.

Ivan wanted to check that everything was fine. He followed Gabriel quietly.

Ivan wanted to check that everything was fine, **so** he followed Gabriel quietly.

The conjunctions *because* and *so* are used to indicate the reason why the action in the sentences take place. They are also used to join two sentences.

Some other common conjunctions that show reason are *since* and *therefore*.

B. Join these pairs of sentences using the conjunctions given in brackets.

1. I did not go to the picnic. I was unwell. (so)
2. It is raining cats and dogs. We should stay indoors. (because)
3. Kusha is only fourteen years old. She cannot apply for a driver's licence. (therefore)
4. Pradipta borrowed five books from the library. He was going for a three-week long vacation. (since)
5. My cousins and I plan to go swimming in the morning. We are sleeping early tonight. (so)

Study Skills

Spelling

words with *-ary*, *-ery* and *-ory*

Words that end with *-ary*, *-ery* and *-ory* are often misspelt, with these suffixes being used incorrectly.

Look at the following table which shows some words that end with the three suffixes.

Words ending with *-ary*	Words ending with *-ery*	Words ending with *-ory*
imaginary	bakery	preparatory
secondary	misery	laboratory
necessary	eatery	explanatory

Fill in the blanks with the correct words.

1. The ______________ (discovery/discovary) of penicillin was a big step in medicine.
2. The ______________ (secretory/secretary) reminded his boss about the meeting.
3. The cricket ______________ (commentery/commentary) kept us glued to the radio.
4. The bank manager was accused of ______________. (bribary/bribery)
5. We will be studying about the ______________ (respiratery/respiratory) system today.
6. The cook prepared a ______________ (satisfactary/satisfactory) meal for the guests.

Listening

listening for information

Listen to a news report and complete the sentences.

1. Since mid-December, cold wave conditions have continued in ________________.
2. The day temperatures remain ________________.
3. ________________ have added to the cold conditions.
4. The Meteorological Department has said ________________.
5. ________________ are being asked to seek shelter in ________________.

Speaking

role play: expressing emotions

21ST CENTURY Social Skills

Imagine that a new student has joined your class. You find that your best friend spends most of her time with her. How would you feel in such a situation? Would you feel jealousy or hurt, or would you be happy that she has found another friend? Enact a dialogue with your partner on the topic.

Useful words and phrases

- Can we ...
- I think you ...
- Couldn't we both ...
- Let's all be ...

You may start like this:

You: Hi ________, can we talk for sometime?

Your friend: Oh, sure! What's the matter? Why do you look so serious?

Writing

describing people

Read this short description of Ivan.

Ivan was a **village peasant** who had everything that he needed to lead a comfortable life. He was a **strong fellow**. He was a **dutiful son** because he took care of his old father. He was **ashamed** of his actions after half the village was burnt down due to his fight with Gabriel.

When we describe someone, we write about their physical features, appearance, occupation, and the things that they have. We also use adjectives to talk about their behaviour, qualities and personality.

Write short descriptions of two characters from the story – Gabriel and Ivan's father, referring to their physical appearance, occupations, behaviour and personality. You can use your imagination to add details.

wise	unforgiving	old
ill-tempered	impatient	prudent
cautious	kind-hearted	quarrelsome
weak	sensitive	regretful

Explore More

Read the book *The Hitopadesha*, a collection of fables, translated from the original Sanskrit by G. L. Chandiramani, which gives worldly wisdom and advice for living as a useful member of the society.

Watch the 2009 film *Coraline* directed by Henry Selick. It is about a girl named Coraline, who moves into a new apartment building with unusual neighbours and a gateway to a secret world.

Listen to the 1992 song 'Heal the World' written and sung by Michael Jackson. It is about the importance of living together peacefully and making the world a better place, both for ourselves and future generations.

narrative poem

12

The Palki Song

Satyendranath Dutta

Curricular Goals

- develop a comprehensive range of vocabulary in different contexts
- explore the structure of various literary devices
- organize ideas and information to write for an intended purpose

Competencies

- can use *-ing* adjectives in sentences
- can understand and use alliteration
- can write a short descriptive paragraph

Reading

a *India is a country made up of villages whose landscapes change completely from state to state. Read this poem which describes the sights and sounds of villages in Bengal in the past, as seen by someone travelling through them in a palanquin or palki. Have you travelled through or stayed in an Indian village?*

INDIA FOCUS

The palki moves
And passes by,
A **haze** of heat
Beneath the sky!

Silent village
People run
With **torso** bare
In **scorching** sun!

Vendors on their
Wooden seat
Snooze and doze
In noonday heat.

Flies flitter,
As they hum
And hover on
The **milky scum.**

Roughly clad
The walkers run –
The market's closed
In midday sun.

Sniffing dust,
The doggies **hark** –
Listless, and
Too weak to bark!

Cows **barge in**
Without a **care**.
The scent of mangoes
Fills the air!

The palki moves,
And swings and goes –
Like a dancer[1]
On her toes!

Literary term

1. This is a **simile**. The movement of the *palki* is compared to the light-footed movement of a dancer using the word *like*.

haze: air which is difficult to see through because it has particles of dust and water
torso: upper part of the human body
scorching: very hot
snooze: have a short, light sleep, especially during the day
milky scum: (here) the layer that forms on milk as it cools
hark: listen
listless: without energy or enthusiasm
barge in: enter a place suddenly interrupting somebody's work or conversation
care: worry

The bearers six,
So **sprightly**, strong –
Towards the field
They move along.

The field – a flaming
Copper plate,
Too hot to walk –
A fiery **grate**!

Up and down
They step and cave,
Tossing like
A breaking wave!

A ship on land[2]
That forward **flits**
On oar-like legs
Of bearers six!

The **drowsy** jutes
Are dusky green,
And paddy fields
Now bare and clean.

'Beware!' they cry
And take a turn.
The bearers six
See how they run!

Kites in air,
The cows in shed,
There's the village
Right ahead.

Wearing beads,
The **hermit** tall
Plasters mud
Upon the wall.

The farmer's boy
Looks on in **awe**
From the rooftop
Made of straw.

A butterfly
So yellow, bright
Steps on blossoms,
Treading light!

Who's the **damsel**?
Who can say?
At the pond
She **toils** away –

Scrubbing clean
Her pots and pans,
She pats her clothes
With dirty hands!

Literary term

2. This is a **metaphor**. The *palki* is compared to a ship which moves on land, without using the words *as* or *like*. The bearers' legs are like oars that move it forward.

Which two crops are grown in the village?

sprightly: lively, full of energy
grate: framework of metal bars in a fireplace, which holds the coal or wood
flits: moves along rapidly and lightly
drowsy: sleepy
hermit: a person who lives alone, away from people and cities
awe: feeling of surprise and respect when seeing something wonderful
treading light: (here) walking carefully
damsel: a young, unmarried woman
toils: works very hard

The palki's here?
Where can it be?
The naked toddler
Runs to see!

Hear the schoolboys
Read all day –
Moonbeams in
A house of clay!

The school's within
The village store,
Where the teacher sells
His stuff **galore**!

A ruined house,
An empty **bay** –
Where grazing goats
And sparrows stray

The village ends.
Beneath a tree –
A fire burns,
As you can see,

A fresh green leaf
With **sloppy rice**,
Piping hot
And steaming nice!

Crossing now
The village store,
The palki's on the
Field once more!

A grate of copper
Once again –
The bearers run
Or **tramp** in pain!

The meadow's cracked
In scorching sun
The palki moves –
A steady run!

Where is the village school located?

galore: in plenty
bay: a partly enclosed area, used for a particular purpose
sloppy rice: rice porridge made using a variety of sweet-smelling rice and seasonal vegetables
tramp: walk slowly and with regular, heavy steps for a long time

In a Nutshell

Who the palanquin bearers and the people they meet on the journey

What the sights and sounds from a moving palanquin

Where a village in Bengal

When in summer

About the poet

Satyendranath Dutta (1882–1922) was a Bengali poet. He wrote about patriotism and the sufferings of the downtrodden and was known for his use of rhyme and rhythm. Some of his notable collections of poems are *Sabita*, *Sandhiksan* and *Benu o Bina*.

Understanding the Poem

HOTS

A. Complete the mind map about the sights seen from the *palki* as it passes through the village. One is done for you.

- **landscape of the village**
  - **natural scenery**
  - **the marketplace**
  - **people and community**
    - vendors sitting on wooden seats

B. Answer the questions in a few lines.

1. What are the vendors doing?
2. Which season do you think is referred to in the poem? Give examples to support your answer.
3. The poet uses a metaphor to describe the students studying in the village school. Identify and explain them in your own words.
4. What does the poet mean by the line, 'Where the teacher sells/His stuff galore'?

ia **C. Answer the questions as directed.**

1. The poetic device used in the line, 'Flies flitter,/As they hum' is ________________.
2. The movement of the palanquin has been compared to that of a dancer. Write 'true' or 'false'. Correct the statement if it is false. ________________________________
3. Why are the jutes called drowsy?
   a. They are drooping or bent. b. They are sleepy. c. They look tired.
4. What is the damsel doing?
   a. She is washing utensils. b. She is washing clothes.
   c. She is running to see the *palki*.
5. *Up and down/They step and cave,*
   Tossing like/A breaking wave!
   Whose movement is being described in these lines?
   a. the *palki*'s movement b. the *palki* bearers' movement c. the wave's movement

6. *A grate of copper/Once again –*
The bearers run/Or tramp in pain!
What is described as 'a grate of copper'?
a. the *palki* b. the ground c. the village

7. The poem has two pairs of rhyming words in each stanza. Write the rhyming word pairs for any three stanzas.

____

Life Skills and Values

appreciating life

21ST CENTURY Critical Thinking

1. The poem suggests that life in a village is slow and peaceful. Do you agree? Give examples from the poem to support your answer.
2. The poem has a swaying rhythm which is similar to the movement of the palanquin as it is carried along by its bearers. Discuss the idea in class. Take turns to read out lines from the poem which have this effect.

Vocabulary

-ing adjectives

We often use *-ing* words as adjectives to describe a noun. These are formed by adding the suffix *-ing* to verbs.

Examples: 'They step and cave/Tossing like/A **breaking** wave.'
'People run/With torso bare/In **scorching** sun.'

ia **A. Fill in the blanks with suitable adjectives formed by adding *-ing* to the words in the box. You may need to change some of the words.**

shock	bore	annoy	bark	amuse

1. Raghu has an __________ habit of interrupting people when they are talking.
2. The __________ dog disturbed everyone last night.
3. The film was so __________ that we left during the interval.
4. I do not find your jokes __________.
5. Everyone stopped what they were doing after hearing the __________ news.

alliteration

You know that **alliteration** is the use of the same letter or sound at the beginning of words placed close together in a sentence. In poetry, it creates a rhythmic effect.

Examples: A **h**aze of **h**eat/Beneath the sky!
People run/With torso bare/In **s**corching **s**un!

Remember that alliteration is the repetition of sounds, not letters.

King Cane [✓]	ten thirty [x]
('k' and 'c' have the same sound)	('t' and 'th' have different sounds)

B. Read these lines taken from different poems, and underline the alliteration in each.

1. Chicken, chilli, and cheddar cheese / When I munch too much, I always sneeze.
2. That whisper takes the voice. / Of a spirit, speaking to me …
3. Betty Botter bought some butter, / 'But,' she said, 'the butter's bitter …'
4. Why don't you eat ice cream or chocolatey cake! / Oh, slithery, slidery, scaly old snake.
5. While I nodded, nearly napping, suddenly there came a tapping …

Activity

writing short descriptions

The poem describes a market in a village. Visit your local market and write short descriptions of any three elements that catch your eye. You can write about a person, an object or a scene.

Remember the following points:

- When describing something, it is better to use phrases which 'show' rather than 'tell'.

  Example: The line 'The scent of mangoes/Fills the air' makes us think of the sweet smell of mangoes. It is more relatable than saying, 'There were many mangoes.'
- Use words related to the senses (smell, touch, sight, taste, sound) to describe the scene.

Explore More

Read the poem 'The Palanquin Bearers' by Sarojini Naidu, about a young bride travelling in a palanquin. The palanquin bearers sing of the bride's beauty, comparing it to different things.

Listen to the Bengali song 'Palkir Gaan' by Hemanta Mukherjee. It describes the movement of the palanquin.

Project 2

bagless day activity

A. The poem 'The Palki Song' shows the interconnectedness of the village community. Form groups of four and hold 'Connect-with-our-Elders Week' in your families and neighbourhood. During this week, spend time with your grandparents or other elderly people around you and get to know them better.

You may carry out these activities with them:

- Watch a film, television series, or a documentary.
- Play board games.
- Go for a walk with them or run errands for them.
- Help them learn how to operate smartphones or any other electronic devices.

Based on your interactions, fill the given chart as a group:

Name and age	Relationship with you	Activities you did together	Activities they enjoyed the most	Problems they face	Things you learnt from them

Share your findings in the classroom, with each group making a presentation.

B. You read about scorpions and their habits in the chapter 'An Unexpected Guest'.
Work in pairs and collect information about geckos. Create a scrapbook on them and include the following information. Add pictures of various species of geckos as well.

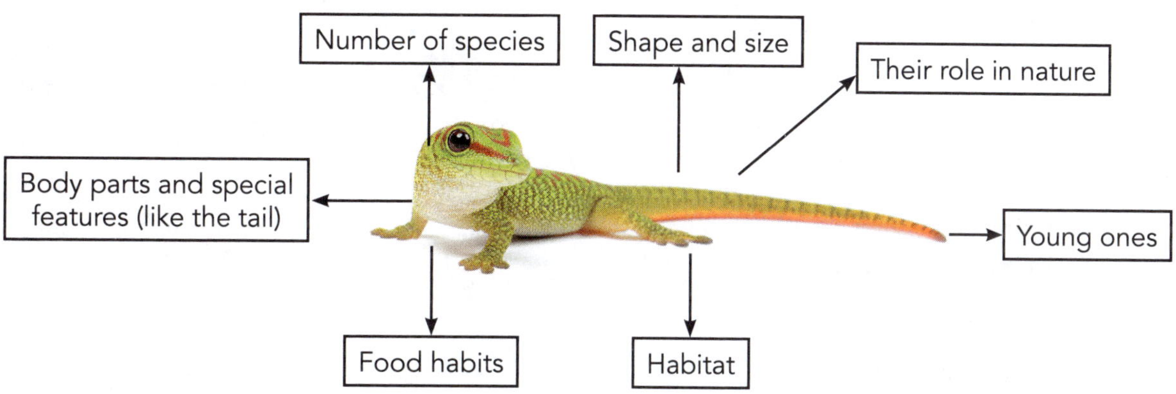

UNIT VII

Food and Celebrations

Warm-up

A. We celebrate various festivals with our friends and family. Read these sentences and identify the Indian festivals.

1. We decorate our homes with lights, light fireworks and share sweets with our friends on ______________.
2. ______________ is a festival when we play with colours to celebrate spring's arrival.
3. During ______________, we watch *Ramlila* performances and Ravana's effigies are burnt.
4. On ______________, children get *eidi* from parents.
5. On ______________, children go on treasure hunts for chocolate eggs and bunnies.
6. During ______________, boat races are held in Kerala.
7. To celebrate their bond, a sister ties a thread on her brother's wrist on ______________.
8. ______________ marks the end of winter, and is celebrated with bonfires, singing and dancing in North India.

B. Yorkshire pudding and Brussels sprouts are two examples of food items named after places. Complete the names of the following food items.

1. Waldorf ______________
2. Bombay ______________
3. ______________ Chettinad
4. Bourbon ______________
5. ______________ toast
6. ______________ delight
7. Malabar ______________
8. Black ______________ cake

(The answers are given on page 156.)

mystery

13 The Theft of the Ruby

Agatha Christie

Curricular Goals

- develop a comprehensive range of vocabulary in various contexts
- recognize basic linguistic aspects and use them in written and oral expression
- use language effectively in other curricular areas to comprehend concepts and share understanding with others
- organize thoughts and opinions to write for an intended purpose

→

Competencies

- can identify words related to celebrations and classify verbs with similar meaning
- can understand perfect and perfect continuous tenses, and use *would* and *used to* to talk about the past
- can enact the story as a play and write a notice

Reading

a *Imagine your family was celebrating a festive occasion, and amidst the gaiety, you find yourself caught in a mystery. Read on to find out what might happen next.*

A band of young people were chatting **companionably** together, while the big logs crackled merrily in the fireplace. Old Miss Endicott, known as Aunt Emily, looked on fondly at Jean, Nancy Cardell, the two younger boys, Johnson and Eric, their friend Charlie Pease, and Evelyn Haworth. Evelyn was **engaged** to Oscar Levering, who was also visiting with his sister. Then her eyes wandered to her eldest nephew, Roger, who sat **morosely** silent, looking at Evelyn.

Seated among them was a little man with a curious egg-shaped head and fierce **upstanding** moustaches. The famous detective Hercule Poirot had joined them for Christmas.

'Real Christmas weather!' cried Johnnie, looking out of the window.

'Let's make a snowman!' suggested Jean.

They all disappeared like a **whirlwind**[1].

Poirot noticed that Evelyn was staring at the fire, twisting a ring on her left hand. She hadn't gone out with the rest.

'You seem lost, madam,' said Poirot gently.

'I am so miserable, Mr Poirot,' she answered. A year ago, Evelyn Haworth's mother had fallen seriously ill and needed an expensive operation. Desperate and without money, Evelyn had accepted Mr Levering's marriage proposal.

Literary term

1. This is an example of a **simile**, where the speed with which the people disappeared is compared to the movement of a whirlwind, which also comes and disappears very fast.

companionably: in a friendly way
morosely: gloomily
engaged: having agreed to marry somebody
upstanding: straight, upright
whirlwind: a very strong wind that moves fast in a spinning movement

'Mr Levering kept his word. The operation was performed and my mother is now well and strong again; and I – I am to marry Mr Levering after Christmas.'

'I see,' said Mr Poirot. 'But Roger also cared for you. And now he has come home to find his dream shattered.'

Evelyn didn't reply, but did not disagree.

At that moment, the door opened. Mr Levering stood on the threshold.

'Come out for a **stroll**, Evelyn,' he said.

She rose **listlessly**.

Poirot asked politely: 'Madam Levering, she is still unwell?'

'Yes, I'm sorry to say that my sister is still in bed.'

In the snow-covered grounds, Levering and Evelyn met the others.

'What do you think of the great detective, Evelyn?' Jean cried out.

'We have a real detective in the house!' said Charlie, 'I wish there could be a murder, too.'

'I've got an idea,' cried Jean. 'Let's enact a murder – a **spoof**, I mean.'

Five voices began to talk at once about the plan.

'We can use red paint.'

'Nancy can be it; she's got those **scarlet** pyjamas.'

'Let's ask Graves for some paint.'

The group **stampeded** back to the house.

Back inside, Levering asked Roger, 'Why so **glum**, Endicott?'

'I was just wondering,' he said quietly, 'what brings Mr Poirot here.'

Levering seemed **taken aback**; but at that moment the big gong rang, and everybody went in for Christmas dinner. The **Squire**, Aunt Emily's brother, **carved** rapidly, and everyone fell on the **turkey**. Graves, the butler, appeared, bearing aloft a gigantic plum pudding, covered in flames. A **hullabaloo** broke out.

Cross-curricular Corner

Hercule Poirot, a fictional Belgian detective, is one of the most famous characters created by Agatha Christie. Poirot left Belgium for England as a refugee during World War I. He is supported in many cases by his friend, Captain Arthur Hastings. He is known for using his brain ('the little grey cells') and 'order and method' while solving cases.

Plum pudding was originally made with plums. Nowadays, the pudding is made with raisins, but the name has not changed. This pudding is especially made for Christmas, and as part of the tradition, every member of the family gets to stir the pudding when it is being made and make a wish.

Who had scarlet pyjamas?

stroll: walk
listlessly: not in an enthusiastic manner
spoof: a trick played on someone as a joke
scarlet: bright red
stampeded: rushed
glum: sad
taken aback: surprised
Squire: a man of high social position, a chief landowner
carved: cut a large piece of cooked meat into smaller pieces
turkey: a large bird, popular food on festive days like Christmas
hullabaloo: loud noise and confusion

'Quick, my piece is going out. **Buck up**, Graves; unless it's still burning, I shan't get my wish.'

Suddenly the Squire's face became purple and his hand went to his mouth.

'Emily!' he roared. 'Why do you let the cook put glass in the puddings?'

'Glass?' cried Miss Endicott, astonished.

The Squire dropped the piece of glass into a small **finger bowl** of water, placed there for the **sixpences** and other trinkets found in the **trifle**. He rinsed it and held it up.

Mr Poirot took it from him and examined it attentively. It was a big red stone, the colour of a ruby.

'Is it real? A ruby that size would be worth thousands, wouldn't it, Mr Poirot?' said Jean.

'But how did it get into the pudding?' asked Miss Endicott.

After dinner, Poirot paid a visit to the cook and found that the pudding had been made three days ago. Everyone had come out into the kitchen to have a stir and wish, an old custom. But this wasn't the Christmas pudding, which was always boiled in a **china** mould with **holly leaves**. However, today the kitchen maid accidentally broke the mould, with the pudding in it. So, the one in the aluminium dish was served instead. Mr Poirot thanked the cook for this information and left, smiling a little to himself. The fingers of his right hand played with something in his pocket.

'Mr Poirot! Do wake up! Something dreadful has happened!' screamed Johnnie the following morning. Mr Poirot arose, and followed Johnnie down the stairs. Everyone was gathered around the door into the garden. Jean came forward and pointed dramatically through the open door. The snow-covered landscape looked ghostly in the early dawn except for a splash of brigh scarlet. Nancy Cardell lay motionless on the snow, wearing scarlet silk pyjamas. From her left side rose the **hilt** of a dagger.

Poirot went out into the snow. But he didn't go directly to the girl. He followed the footprints – of a man and a woman – that led to the spot. The man's footprints went away in the opposite direction, alone. Poirot stood on the path, **reflectively**. Suddenly Mr Levering burst out of the house.

'Good God!' he cried excitedly. 'What's this?'

'It looks,' said Mr Poirot **grimly**, 'like murder. You must send for the police.'

buck up: hurry up

finger bowl: a small bowl containing water for rinsing the fingers after meal

sixpences: small silver coins, used in Britain till 1971

trifle: a dessert made of layers of sponge cake, jelly, fruit and custard, and usually covered with cream

china: (here) porcelain or ceramic

holly leaves: leaves of an evergreen shrub usually used for Christmas decorations

hilt: handle

reflectively: thoughtfully

grimly: very seriously

There was a pause, and then Johnnie came forward.

'Mr Poirot, I hope you won't be too mad with us. It's all a joke, you know,' he declared. 'Say Nancy, get up! Don't lie there all day.'

But the figure on the ground did not move. Suddenly a feeling of **dread** came over the boy. Poirot walked over the snow, waving the others back. The boy followed him, frightened. Poirot knelt down by the girl and **signed** to Johnnie.

'Feel her hand and pulse.'

Johnnie bent forward. Nancy's hand had gone stiff and cold, and no pulse was to be found.

'She's dead!' he gasped. 'But how? Why?'

'I wonder,' Mr Poirot said. Suddenly he **unclasped** her other hand. In Nancy's palm was a red stone that winked and flashed forth fire.

Mr Poirot quickly put his hand into his pocket, and came away empty.

'The ruby,' said Johnnie. Then, as Mr Poirot bent to examine the dagger, and the **stained** snow, he cried out, 'Surely it can't be blood, Mr Poirot. It's only paint.'

'You are right,' he said quietly. 'It's only paint. Now, did she eat or drink anything this morning?'

'She had a cup of tea,' said the boy. 'Mr Levering made it for her. He's got a **spirit lamp** in his room.'

'Such a handy thing,' Mr Levering answered. 'My sister's been glad of it this visit. There's no need to worry the help all the time.'

At that moment, Mr Poirot's eyes fell to Mr Levering's feet. He was wearing carpet slippers.

'You have changed your boots, I see,' he said. Levering stared at him. 'Now, for the police.'

'I'll go,' cried Levering. 'It won't take me a minute to put my boots on.'

He disappeared into the house.

'Until the police come, nothing here must be touched. Shall we go inside? I have a little history to **recount** to you,' said Mr Poirot.

'A precious ruby once belonged to a very celebrated man. He came to London, where he met a pretty young lady. Soon after, the lady disappeared with a historic ruby which had belonged to his family for generations. This man came to me. "Recover for me my ruby," he says. I know that this lady has a brother, and together they have tricked many people. I know where they are staying for Christmas.

By the kindness of Mr Endicott, I too become a guest there. But when this lady hears that I am arriving, she is alarmed. She knows that I am after the ruby. She needs to hide it immediately in a safe place; and where but in a plum-pudding! She is stirring with the rest, you see, and she pops it into a pudding bowl of aluminium that is different from the others. By a strange chance, that pudding came to be used on Christmas Day.'

The tragedy forgotten for the moment, everyone stared at him open-mouthed. Evelyn rose with a cry, her eyes fixed on Poirot.

signed: (here) called by using a hand movement
dread: fearing that something bad is going to happen
unclasped: loosened the grip
stained: covered with a mark that is difficult to remove
spirit lamp: a lamp that burns industrial or medical alcohol instead of oil
recount: tell somebody about something

The detective continued, 'I expect that Mr Levering and his sister will not return.'

'Did he kill Nancy?' whispered Jean.

Poirot rose, walking back to the scene of the crime.

But when the others reached the spot, they gasped. The snow was smooth and unbroken.

'Most extraordinary,' said Mr Poirot, '*The Mystery of the Disappearing Body*.' His eyes twinkled gently.

Jean came up to him in sudden suspicion.

'Mr Poirot, you have been spoofing us all the time, haven't you?'

'I knew about your little plot,' Mr Poirot smiled, 'and so arranged a little **counterplot** of my own. Ah, here is Nancy.'

Nancy Cardell appeared, her eyes shining.

'I asked **Mademoiselle** Nancy to act a part for me. She persuaded Mr Levering to make her a cup of tea, and managed that he should be the one chosen to leave footprints on the snow. So when the time came, and he thought that she was really dead, I could frighten him with it.'

'After everyone went inside,' Nancy began, 'he came down with his sister, snatched the ruby out of my hand, and off they went **post-haste**. Goodness Mr Poirot, my arm hurts still after that **tourniquet** you made me put on it.'

'So the ruby is lost?' cried Eric.

'Feel in my left pocket.'

Jean thrust in an eager hand, and drew it out again with a squeal of **triumph**. The great ruby in its crimson splendour was there for all to see.

'You see,' smiled Poirot, 'the other was a paste **replica** I had brought with me from London.'

counterplot: a plan to prevent another plan from working
Mademoiselle: Miss, in French
post-haste: with great speed
tourniquet: a strip of cloth usually tied tightly round a limb to control the circulation of blood
triumph: a great success, achievement or victory
replica: an exact copy

In a Nutshell

What recovery of a precious ruby that was stolen

Who the thieves: Mr Levering and his sister

How Hercule Poirot arranged a plot to get the ruby back.

Where at Mr Endicott's house

When on Christmas day

About the author

Agatha Christie (1890–1976) was an English writer, celebrated for her thrillers and murder mysteries. Her stories usually revolve around her fictional detectives, Hercule Poirot and Miss Marple. *Murder on the Orient Express*, and *And Then There Were None* are some of her famous novels.

Comprehension

A. Complete the flowchart to show the sequence of events in the story.

1. A group of people had gathered for Christmas celebrations, including the famous ______________ ______________.
2. The young people were excited and decided ______________ ______________.
3. At dinner, the plum pudding was brought in, but then the Squire discovered ______________ ______________.
4. The cook informed Poirot that the original pudding ______________ ______________.
5. Next morning, they found ______________, lying dead in the snow. Poirot noticed ______________.
6. Johnnie realized that instead of acting, Nancy ______________ ______________.
7. They found the ______________ in her hand which Poirot ______________. Mr Levering offered to ______________.
8. Poirot told everyone that ______________ ______________ ______________ ______________.
9. It was also revealed that Nancy was ______________ and the ruby ______________ ______________ ______________.

B. Answer the questions as directed.

HOTS

1. *Poirot noticed that Evelyn was staring at the fire, twisting a ring on her left hand.* What does Evelyn's action in this line tell us?
   a. She was fascinated by the fire.
   b. She was upset about having accepted Mr Levering's proposal.
   c. She was uncomfortable because the ring was tight on her finger.

2. *'I knew about your little plot,' Mr Poirot smiled, 'and so arranged a little counterplot of my own.'* Why do think Poirot arranged a counterplot?
    a. He wanted to catch the thief who had stolen the red ruby.
    b. He wanted to teach everyone a lesson.
    c. He wanted to participate in the family's Christmas tradition of solving a mystery.
3. *The detective continued, 'I expect that Mr Levering and his sister will not return.'* Why did he not expect them to return?
    a. They knew that Poirot had figured out that they were the thieves.
    b. They thought that they had successfully stolen the ruby.
    c. They were travelling together.
4. *They all disappeared like a whirlwind.* Name the figure of speech being used here.
5. Hercule Poirot used the family's fake plot to uncover the identity of the real thieves. What impression of Poirot do you get from the story?
    a. He was sensitive and funny.
    b. He got lucky and found the real thieves.
    c. He was two steps ahead of everyone else and was able to outwit both the thieves and the holiday-makers.

Life Skills and Values

festive traditions

1. What are the different Christmas traditions mentioned by the author?
2. Do you have festive traditions in your family? Note down any two and mention why they are followed.

Vocabulary

words related to celebrations

A. Find eight words related to celebrations in the word grid.

P	U	B	I	T	U	A	O	T	G	V	I	S	S	P
A	C	F	R	A	B	I	T	I	O	N	N	R	V	R
R	C	L	H	Z	B	B	R	F	E	A	S	T	Y	E
T	E	S	F	X	S	C	O	S	T	U	M	E	K	S
Y	R	U	S	M	G	B	E	F	E	O	L	D	J	E
Y	E	B	I	R	T	H	D	A	Y	N	Q	R	C	N
E	M	N	K	E	V	P	L	R	D	H	Q	H	G	T
C	O	B	L	W	G	A	T	H	E	R	I	N	G	S
F	N	B	A	N	Q	U	E	T	K	A	X	N	L	P
A	Y	G	J	A	Z	R	Q	Q	R	W	X	D	T	M

Read these sentences.

'Emily!' he **roared**. 'Why do you let the cook put glass in the puddings?'

'Glass?' **cried** Miss Endicott, astonished.

'Mr Poirot! Do wake up! Something dreadful has happened!' **screamed** Johnnie.

The verbs in bold in these sentences have similar meanings.

ia **B. Classify the verbs according to the base verb they share their meanings with and write them in the correct columns.**

sense	murmur	listen	observe	notice	chat
glance	believe	catch	utter	understand	whisper
spot	say	think	look		

speak	see	hear	feel

Grammar

tenses: perfect and perfect continuous

The **present perfect tense** is used to talk about an action completed in the recent past but whose effects still remain. It is formed with *has/have* + *-ed/-d/-t/-en* form of the verb.

Example: Something dreadful **has happened**.

The **present perfect continuous tense** is used to talk about an action that started in the past but is still going on at the time of speaking. It is formed with *has/have been* + *-ing* form of the verb.

Example: You **have been spoofing** us all the time.

The **past perfect tense** is used to talk about a past action that was completed before another past action began. It is formed with *had* + *-ed/-d/-t/-en* form of the verb.

Example: She **had prepared** the pudding three days ago.

The **past perfect continuous tense** is used to talk about an action that took place in the past and continued for a period of time before it was completed. It is formed with *had been* + *-ing* form of the verb.

Example: Nancy **had been lying** in the snow for quite some time.

ia **A. Complete the sentences using the correct perfect or perfect continuous form of the given verbs.**

1. The parrot ______________________ (learn) several new words today.
2. Jake was hospitalized because he ______________________ (break) his leg.
3. She ______________________ (try) to solve the crossword for half an hour.
4. You ______________________ (study) since morning, haven't you?
5. I ______________________ (climb) this mountain for over two hours now.
6. The old lady ______________________ (feed) her dog by noon.

describing the past using *would* and *used to*

We use *used to* and *would* to talk about repeated actions in the past.

Read these sentences.

Everyone **would** come out to the kitchen to have a stir and make a wish, an old custom.

The Squire, Aunt Emily's brother, **used to** carve the turkey for Christmas dinner.

We use *would* to talk about past events.

We use *used to* to describe old habits, and past states.

ia **B. Read this paragraph from the diary of a basketball player and fill in the blanks with *would* or *used to*.**

I ______________________ be a sporty person in high school. I ______________________ wear high-power glasses at the time, so I thought there was no chance that I ______________________ be selected for the school team. Little did I know how surprised I ______________________ be. On my first day of training, I met the man who ______________________ be my lifelong coach and mentor. I ______________________ do a lot of weight training earlier, but he ______________________ change my exercise routine to one that improved my fitness more. I ______________________ be afraid of not winning every tournament always, but my outlook changed, thanks to his guidance.

Study Skills

Dictionary Skills

words of French origin

Look at these words from the story.

curious **disagree** **trifle** **haste**

These are English words which have their origins in the French language.

Use a dictionary to find the meanings of these words of French origin.

1. chef
2. petite
3. ballad
4. en route
5. caramel
6. regime

Listening

listening for facts

Listen to a passage on the celebration of *Basanta Utsav* (spring festival) and write whether these statements are true (T) or false (F). Correct the false statements.

1. The name *Visva Bharati* highlights the coming together of the world with India. ☐
2. *Basanta Utsav* takes place in autumn. ☐
3. *Aamro Kunjo* is a garden of orange trees. ☐
4. Women wear *palash* flowers. ☐
5. Tagore compared the flowers with bright red rubies. ☐
6. People hold colours in baskets woven with ribbons. ☐
7. They dance to the tunes of *Rabindrsangeet*. ☐

Dictation

You will now listen to a short passage on fish and chips. Write it down. Each sentence will be repeated twice. Listen carefully and be careful not to make any spelling errors.

Speaking

enacting the story as a play

Collaboration | Creativity

Work in groups and enact the story as a play, following the given steps.

1. Divide the events of the story into three scenes.
2. Make a list of the characters and decide which character each student would play. Choose someone to be the narrator, to hold the events of the play together.
3. Use lines from the story to prepare dialogues for the characters.
4. Use the front of the classroom as a makeshift stage with ordinary objects used as props.

Writing

notice

A **notice** is a formal written communication to inform a group of people about an event or to convey important information. It is short and contains only the essential details of the event.

Look at this format for writing a notice.

Name of the organization → LITTLE GEMS INTERNATIONAL SCHOOL

Write the word 'NOTICE' → **NOTICE**

Date → 15 June 2024

Subject → Fancy Dress Competition

Body of the notice → A fancy dress competition is being conducted on 22 June 2024 in the school auditorium. All interested students are requested to dress up as a character of their choice. The results will be announced by the judges at 12:30 p.m.

Name of the writer → Asiya Chowdhury

Designation of the writer → Teacher-in-charge, Annual Day

Imagine that you are the organizer of the theatre club in your school. The club plans to put up a play based on the story 'The Theft of the Ruby'. Write a notice inviting interested students to audition for the play. Mention the date, time and venue for the audition.

Explore More

Read the short story 'The Adventure of the Blue Carbuncle' by Arthur Conan Doyle about how Sherlock Holmes, the celebrated detective, solves the mystery of a priceless gem turning up inside a Christmas goose left on a London street.

Watch the 2016 Disney movie *Zootopia* directed by Byron Howard and Richard Moore. It is about a new officer in the Zootopia Police Department, Judy Hopps, who decides to solve a murder to prove her abilities to her superiors.

Listen to the popular Christmas carol 'Joy to the World'.

light verse

14 I Wave Good-bye When Butter Flies

Jack Prelutsky

Curricular Goals

- develop vocabulary by listening to and reading a variety of texts and other content areas
- use strategies to organize ideas and information to write for an intended purpose and audience

Competencies

- can use homophones and identify puns
- can create an advertisement

Reading

a *Have you ever looked at certain words and thought about how they might have been coined? Read this funny poem in which everyday things take on extraordinary qualities through the use of puns.*

A pun is a clever and amusing use of a word or phrase with two meanings, or of words with the same sound but different meanings.

I wave good-bye when butter flies[1]
and cheer a boxing match,
I've often watched my pillow fight[2],
I've sewn a cabbage patch,
I like to dance at basket balls
or lead a rubber band,
I've **marvelled** at a **spelling bee**,
I've helped a peanut stand.
It's possible a pencil points[3],
but does a **lemon drop**?
Does coffee break or **chocolate kiss**,
and will a soda pop?
I share my milk with drinking straws,
my meals with chewing gum,
and should I see my pocket change,
I'll hear my **kettle drum**.
It makes me sad when lettuce leaves,
I laugh when **dinner rolls**,

Literary terms

1. This is a **pun** on the word 'butterflies'. It has two meanings here:
   a. colourful flying insects,
   b. the act of butter flying in the air.
2. This is an example of **personification**. The pillow has been imagined as a person who is having a fight. This device has been used by the poet frequently in this poem.
3. This is an example of **alliteration**, as the 'p' sound is repeated in words placed one after the other.

marvelled: to be impressed by something

spelling bee: a competition in which people have to spell difficult words

lemon drop: a small, hard, lemon-flavoured candy

chocolate kiss: a type of chocolate candy

kettledrum: a large bowl-shaped drum which can be tuned to play a particular note

dinner rolls: small round pieces of bread provided with a meal

I wonder if the kitchen sinks
and if a salad bowls,
I've listened to a diamond ring,
I've waved a football fan,
and if a chimney sweeps the floor,
I'm sure the garbage can.

Cross-curricular Corner

In America, a fizzy drink is called a *soda pop*. The same items have different British and American names. *Fries* are called *chips* in American English, whereas *chips* in American English are called *crisps* in British English.

In a Nutshell

What a clever poem with multiple meanings of the same word being used

How The poet uses puns.

About the poet

Jack Prelutsky (born 1940) is an American writer of children's poetry. He has published over fifty poetry collections, including *Nightmares: Poems to Trouble Your Sleep*, and *Behold the Bold Umbrellaphant and Other Poems*. His works have been translated into many languages.

Understanding the Poem

A. Choose the correct answers.

1. What is the implied meaning of 'a boxing match' in the poem?
   a. a box of matches
   b. a match stick that is in a boxing match
   c. a boxing contest
2. The poet dances at 'basket balls'. Which 'balls' does the poet mean here?
   a. formal social events where people dance
   b. round objects used in games
   c. rounded part in human body where the toes join the foot
3. *It's possible a pencil points...*
   Which poetic device has not been used in the above line?
   a. alliteration
   b. simile
   c. personification
4. In the line 'I share my milk with drinking straws', the pun is in the word ______
   a. 'share'. The poet says that he has milk with drinking straws.
   b. 'straws'. The straws are imagined as both drinking straws and as the dried yellowish stalks from crops.
   c. 'drinking'. The straws are imagined as people drinking milk.
5. The tone of the poem is ______
   a. scary and gloomy.
   b. sad and serious.
   c. clever and happy.
6. The poet wonders if a salad bowls. What does the poet mean by 'bowl' here?
   a. a round container with an uncovered top
   b. leave the field during a game of cricket because the bowler has hit the wicket with the ball
   c. bowls the ball in a game like baseball or cricket

B. Answer the questions with reference to context.

1. *I've marvelled at a spelling bee,*
   I've helped a peanut stand.
   a. Why, according to the poem, is a spelling bee something to marvel at?
   b. What is an actual spelling bee?
   c. Explain the pun used in the second line.
2. *I share my milk with drinking straws,*
   my meals with chewing gum,
   and should I see my pocket change,
   I'll hear my kettle drum.
   a. What are the everyday things the poet talks about in the quoted lines?
   b. Explain the pun used in the last two lines.
   c. The poem also uses personification in each of the above lines. Explain any one. (hint: They are the puns.)

Life Skills and Values

humour, appreciating everyday things

21ST CENTURY Critical Thinking

1. Did you find the poem funny? Give two examples and state why they make you laugh.
2. How does the poet use wordplay to create funny visuals for us? Do you think the poem helps us look at ordinary things in a new light?

Vocabulary

homophones

Look at these words.

bee (a black and yellow flying insect that can sting)

be (to exist)

break (damage or separate into parts)

brake (a device for slowing or stopping a vehicle)

These words are homophones.

Homophones are words that have the same pronunciation but different spellings and meanings.

ia **A. Replace the underlined words with correct homophones to make meaningful sentences.**

1. He placed the <u>flours</u> inside the glass vase.
2. She will <u>right</u> a letter to her sister tomorrow.
3. <u>Witch</u> book do you want to borrow this week?
4. My mother <u>pored</u> me a glass of cold lemonade.
5. This dress is <u>lose</u> and does not fit me at all.
6. My dog <u>stairs</u> at me greedily whenever I open a packet of chips.

You have learnt that a **pun** is a form of word play that uses multiple meanings of a word, or similar-sounding words, to create a humorous effect.

Example: In the line 'I've listened to a diamond ring', the poet makes a pun on the word 'ring'. It has two meanings here:
1. an item of jewellery worn on the finger,
2. the sound of a telephone or a bell.

ia **B. Underline the pun in the given lines from the poem and explain the two meanings of each word.**

Pun	Meaning 1	Meaning 2
1. I wave good-bye when butter flies		
2. I've sewn a cabbage patch		
3. lead a rubber band		
4. will a soda pop?		
5. It makes me sad when lettuce leaves		
6. I wonder if the kitchen sinks		

Activity

creating an advertisement — 21st Century: Creativity, Media Literacy

An advertisement is created for the promotion of a product or service or even an event. Create an advertisement for butter and cheese. Show your advertisement in class as a presentation. It should have the following points:

- an imaginary brand name
- adjectives to make the product sound attractive
- nutritional information
- its price
- introductory offers
- an illustration or photo of the product
- a tagline (This is a phrase that comes at the beginning or the end, and is meant to be amusing or easy to remember).

Explore More

Read the poem 'The ABC' by Spike Milligan. It is a funny conversation among the alphabets who come alive and talk about various rules of language.

Watch the 2007 Disney film *Ratatouille* by Brad Bird. It is about a young rat, Remy, who is extremely fond of food and he wants to become a chef.

Listen to 'The Pun Song' written by Don Black from the 1972 film *Alice's Adventures in Wonderland*. It is a funny song that is sung at the Mad Hatter's tea party.

UNIT VIII

History

Warm-up

A. War has always been a sad part of history. Find the antonyms of the given words related to war in the grid and circle them.

21ST CENTURY Critical Thinking

1. lose
2. peace
3. cowardice
4. defend
5. free
6. victory

E	O	V	X	C	M	E	M	A	G	L	Y	F	J	P
X	D	D	R	S	V	E	Z	C	A	P	T	I	V	E
C	N	H	A	U	B	K	E	Q	I	H	P	C	Y	P
D	J	Q	J	Y	D	F	E	S	N	T	Y	K	P	R
R	K	M	G	O	E	O	P	S	D	O	R	F	W	X
I	P	M	A	G	F	B	R	A	V	E	R	Y	J	F
U	V	M	L	A	E	P	M	S	A	T	T	A	C	K
G	P	O	X	A	A	V	V	P	N	I	P	X	F	E
Y	O	M	K	L	T	W	A	R	C	P	K	X	Z	J
S	T	D	V	P	Y	Z	G	R	E	P	C	O	N	X

B. Match the historical figures with their descriptions.

INDIA FOCUS — 21ST CENTURY Information Literacy

Historical figure	Description
1. Rani Lakshmibai	a. He is believed to have been the greatest king of the Tamil Chola dynasty, during whose reign (985–1014 AD) the empire became a leader in military, administrative and cultural achievements in South Asia.
2. Emperor Ashoka	b. He became the third Mughal emperor, succeeding his father, Humayun, in 1556. Under his rule, the Mughal Empire grew vastly in size and wealth.
3. Emperor Akbar	c. She was the Queen of Jhansi who fought bravely against the British forces and was a leading figure in the Indian Rebellion of 1857.
4. Rajaraja I	d. He was a sixteenth-century saint and poet, who lived in present-day Varanasi, Uttar Pradesh. He was the author of the *Hanuman Chalisa* and the epic *Ramcharitmanas*.
5. Tulsidas	e. He became the third emperor of the Mauryan Empire in 268 BC. After seeing the terrifying bloodshed in the Kalinga War, he decided to follow the path of non-violence and adopted Buddhism.

15 The Christmas Truce

Aaron Shepard

Curricular Goals

- develop a comprehensive range of vocabulary in various contexts
- recognize basic linguistic aspects and use them in expression
- communicate effectively using language skills for description, analysis, and response
- express experiences and emotions on the various aspects of their surroundings in writing

Competencies

- can use contextual words and idioms related to the army
- can identify different types of sentences, and use prepositions of place and time
- can pronounce words with silent consonants
- can narrate a chain story, and write a diary entry

Reading

a *War can often put people who would have been friends on opposite sides. Read this play in which English and German soldiers, guarding the* ***trenches*** *on opposite sides of the border, set their differences aside for one special occasion. The play is imagined in the form of letters being read out by four English soldiers who are in the trenches.*

Characters

Soldier 1 **Soldier 3**

Soldier 2 **Soldier 4**

Soldier 1 *(to audience)*: Christmas Day, 1914. Dear mother,

Soldier 2 *(to audience)*: My darling Meg,

Soldier 3 *(to audience)*: My good friend Charles,

Soldier 4 *(to audience)*: My dear sister Janet,

Soldier 1: It is 2:00 in the morning and most of our men are asleep in their **dugouts**.

Soldier 2: Yet I could not sleep myself before writing to you of the wonderful events of Christmas Eve.

Soldier 3: In truth, what happened seems almost like a fairy tale, and if I hadn't been through it myself, I would hardly believe it.

Cross-curricular Corner

World War I began in 1914 with the assassination of Archduke Franz Ferdinand of Austria-Este in Sarajevo. It was fought between Germany, Austria-Hungary, Bulgaria and the Ottoman Empire who formed the Central powers, and Great Britain, France, Russia, Japan, Italy, Romania and the United States who formed the Allied powers. Advanced military technologies and trench warfare caused destruction of life on a scale never seen before. The war ended in 1918, with the victory of the Allied powers.

truce: an agreement to stop fighting, usually temporarily
trenches: long, deep holes dug in the ground in which soldiers can be protected from enemy attacks
dugouts: rough shelters used by soldiers, made by digging into the ground

Soldier 4: Just imagine: While you and the family sang carols before the fire there in London, I did the same with enemy soldiers here on the battlefields of France!

Soldier 1: As I wrote before, there has been little serious fighting of late. The first battles of the war left so many dead that both sides have held back until replacements could come from home. So, we have mostly stayed in our trenches and waited.

Soldier 2: But what a terrible waiting it has been! Knowing that any moment an **artillery** shell might land and explode beside us in the trench, killing or **maiming** several men. And in daylight not daring to lift our heads above ground, for fear of a **sniper's** bullet.

Where were the soldiers waiting and for what?

Soldier 3: And the rain – it has fallen almost daily. Of course, it collects right in our trenches, where we must **bail** it **out** with pots and pans. And with the rain has come mud – a good foot or more deep.

Soldier 4: It splatters and **cakes** everything, and constantly sucks at our boots. One new **recruit** got his feet stuck in it, and then his hands too when he tried to get out – just like in that American story of the tar baby!

Soldier 1: Through all this, we couldn't help feeling curious about the German soldiers across the way. After all, they faced the same dangers we did, and **slogged** about in the same muck.

Soldier 2: What's more, their first trench was only fifty yards from ours. Between us lay **no-man's-land**, bordered on both sides by barbed wire – yet they were close enough that we sometimes heard their voices.

Soldier 3: Of course, we hated them whenever they killed our friends. But at other times, we joked about them and almost felt we had something in common.

Soldier 4: And now it seems they felt the same.

Cross-curricular Corner

The tar baby features in American author Joel Chandler Harris' *Uncle Remus* stories about Br'er Rabbit, Br'er Fox and other animals. The tar baby is a doll made of tar and turpentine. It was used by Br'er Fox to try to trap Br'er Rabbit. But the cunning rabbit was able to outsmart the fox and escape his trap.

Soldier 1: Just yesterday morning – Christmas Eve Day – we had our first good freeze. Cold as we were, we welcomed it, because at least the mud froze solid.

artillery: large, heavy guns which are often moved on wheels
maiming: causing severe injury like the loss of a limb
sniper: a shooter who shoots from a hidden position
bail out: scoop out water
cakes: (here) covers something with a thick layer that becomes hard when it dries
recruit: a new member of the armed forces
slogged: worked hard at something without stopping
no-man's-land: an area between enemy forces over which no control has been established

Soldier 2: Everything was **tinged** white with frost, while a bright sun shone over all. Perfect Christmas weather.

Soldier 3: During the day, there was little **shelling** or rifle fire from either side. And as darkness fell on our Christmas Eve, the shooting stopped entirely.

Soldier 4: Our first complete silence in months! We hoped it might promise a peaceful holiday, but we didn't count on it. We'd been told the Germans might attack and try to catch us off guard.

Soldier 1: I went to the dugout to rest, and lying on my cot, I must have **drifted** asleep. All at once my friend was shaking me awake, saying, 'Come and see! See what the Germans are doing!' I grabbed my rifle, stumbled out into the trench, and stuck my head cautiously above the sandbags.

Soldier 2: I never hope to see a stranger and more lovely sight. **Clusters** of tiny lights were shining all along the German line, left and right as far as the eye could see.

Soldier 3: 'What is it?' I asked in **bewilderment**, and someone answered, 'Christmas trees!'

Soldier 4: And so it was. The Germans had placed Christmas trees in front of their trenches, lit by candle or lantern like **beacons** of good will.

Soldier 1: And then we heard their voices raised in song. *(singing)* 'Stille nacht, heilige nacht ...'

What did the German carol translate to?

Soldier 2: This carol may not yet be familiar to us in Britain, but one soldier knew it and translated: 'Silent night, holy night.' I've never heard one lovelier – or more meaningful, in that quiet, clear night, its dark softened by a first-quarter moon.

Soldier 3: When the song finished, the men in our trenches **applauded**. Yes, British soldiers applauding Germans!

Soldier 4: Then one of our own men started singing, and we all joined in. *(singing)* 'The first Noel, the angel did say ...'

Soldier 1: In truth, we sounded not nearly as good as the Germans, with their fine **harmonies**. But they responded with enthusiastic applause of their own and then began another. *(singing)* 'O Tannenbaum, o Tannenbaum ...'

Soldier 2: Then we replied. *(singing)* 'O come all ye faithful ...'

Soldier 3: But this time they joined in, singing the words in Latin. *(singing)* 'Adeste fideles ...'

tinged: coloured lightly
shelling: dropping of bombs
drifted: went from one state to another without realizing it
clusters: groups
bewilderment: confusion
beacons: guiding lights
applauded: clapped
harmonies: the pleasant combination of different musical notes at the same time

Soldier 4: British and German **harmonizing** across no-man's-land! I would have thought nothing could be more amazing – but what came next was more so.

Soldier 1: 'English, come over!' we heard one of them shout. 'You no shoot, we no shoot.'

Soldier 2: There in the trenches, we looked at each other in bewilderment. Then one of us shouted jokingly, 'You come over here.'

Soldier 3: To our astonishment, we saw two figures rise from the trench, climb over their barbed wire, and **advance** unprotected across no-man's-land.

Soldier 4: One of them called, 'Send officer to talk.'

Common idioms and proverbs

1. **at the ready:** This idiom means that something is available to be used immediately.
2. **hold your fire:** This idiom means to wait, and be calm. Here, it is a command to not shoot at the soldiers of the other army.

Soldier 1: I saw one of our men lift his rifle at the ready[1], and no doubt others did the same – but our captain called out, 'Hold your fire[2].' Then he climbed out and went to meet the Germans halfway.

Soldier 2: We heard them talking, and a few minutes later, the captain came back with a German glove in his hand! 'We've agreed there will be no shooting before midnight tomorrow,' he announced. 'But sentries are to remain on duty, and the rest of you, stay alert.'

Soldier 3: Across the way, we could make out groups of two or three men starting out of trenches and coming toward us.

Soldier 4: Then some of us were climbing out too, and in minutes more, there we were in no-man's-land, over a hundred soldiers and officers of each side, shaking hands with men we'd been trying to kill just hours earlier!

Soldier 1: Before long a bonfire was built, and around it we **mingled** – British khaki and German grey. I must say, the Germans were the better dressed, with fresh uniforms for the holiday.

Soldier 2: Only a couple of our men knew German, but more of the Germans knew English. I asked one of them why that was.

'Because many have worked in England!' he said. 'Before all this, I was a waiter at the Hotel Cecil. Perhaps I waited on your table!'

What did the German carol translate to?

'Perhaps you did!' I said, laughing.

Soldier 3: One German told me he had a **fiancée** in London and that the war had interrupted their plans for marriage. I said, 'Don't worry. We'll have you beat by Easter, then you can come back and marry her.'

He laughed at that. Then he asked if I'd send her a postcard he'd give me later, and I promised I would.

Soldier 4: Another German had been a porter at Victoria Station. He showed me a picture of his family back in Munich. I told him I should like to meet them someday. He **beamed** and said he would like that very much and gave me his family's address.

Soldier 1: Even those who could not chat could still exchange gifts – our mufflers for their gloves, our tea for their coffee, English food for German food. Badges and buttons from uniforms changed owners,

harmonizing: playing or singing music that combines with the main tune to make a pleasant sound

advance: (here) move forward

mingled: moved among people and talked to them

fiancée: a woman engaged to be married

beamed: had a big happy smile on one's face

and one of our lads walked off with the **infamous** spiked helmet!

Soldier 2: I myself traded a **jackknife** for a leather equipment belt – a fine **souvenir** to show when I get home.

Cross-curricular Corner

German soldiers in the nineteenth and twentieth centuries wore a spiked helmet known as the Pickelhaube or the Pickelhelm.

Soldier 3: Newspapers too changed hands, and the Germans howled with laughter at ours. They assured us that France was finished and Russia nearly beaten too.

Soldier 4: We told them that was nonsense, and one of them said, 'Well, you believe your newspapers and we'll believe ours.'

What did Soldier 2 get in return for his jackknife?

Soldier 1: Clearly they are lied to – yet after meeting these men, I wonder how truthful our own newspapers have been.

Soldier 2: These are not the 'savage **barbarians**' we've read so much about. They are men with homes and families, hopes and fears, principles and, yes, love of country.

Soldier 3: In other words, men like ourselves.

Soldier 1: As it grew late, a few more songs were traded around the fire, and then all joined in for – I am not lying to you – 'Auld Lang Syne.'

Soldier 2: Then we parted with promises to meet again tomorrow.

Soldier 3: And even some talk of a football match.

Soldier 4: I was just starting back to the trenches when an older German clutched my arm. 'My God,' he said, 'why cannot we have peace and all go home?'

I told him gently, 'That you must ask your emperor.'

He looked at me then, **searchingly**. 'Perhaps, my friend. But also, we must ask our hearts.'

infamous: well known for being bad or evil
jackknife: a large knife with a folding blade
souvenir: an object that reminds one of a certain place, occasion, or person
barbarians: people who behave in an uncivilized or cruel manner
searchingly: closely

In a Nutshell

What an agreement to stop fighting for one day

Who between English and German soldiers during World War I

Where on a battlefield in France

When on Christmas Eve

How German soldiers put Christmas trees outside their trenches and both sides started singing Christmas carols.

About the playwright

Aaron Shepard is an award-winning author who is best known for writing children's stories and retellings of folk tales and other traditional literature from all over the world. His notable works are *The Baker's Dozen, The Legend of Lightning Larry* and *The Sea King's Daughter.*

Comprehension

ia HOTS

A. Choose the correct answer.

1. Why did the soldiers welcome the 'first good freeze'?
   - a. It meant that the soldiers would not have to slosh around in the mud.
   - b. It meant that they would get a break from fighting.
   - c. It meant that Christmas was near.
2. *I saw one of our men lift his rifle at the ready, and no doubt others did the same ...*
   What do you understand about the state of mind of the soldiers from this line?
   - a. The soldiers wanted to kill each other.
   - b. The soldiers were doubtful about the other side and could not trust them at first.
   - c. The soldiers wanted to celebrate Christmas.
3. *Newspapers too changed hands, and the Germans <u>howled with laughter</u> at ours.*
   Choose a phrase to replace the underlined words.
   - a. laughed, and made a howling noise like a wolf
   - b. laughed and cried
   - c. laughed loudly
4. What brought the soldiers on the opposite sides together in peace for one night?
   - a. their faith in God
   - b. the poor condition in the trenches
   - c. their tiredness from the long days of fighting
5. Which of the following was not an outcome of the exchange between the English and the German soldiers?
   - a. They realized that they were all human beings with families.
   - b. They gained a deeper, clearer understanding that everyone wants peace.
   - c. They decided to stop fighting and wrote to their superiors about what had happened.

B. Answer the questions in a few lines.

1. Who are the speakers in the play? What were they reading?
2. What made the waiting for the soldiers terrible? How did the weather add to the problems?
3. What incident was being referred to in relation to the tar baby story?
4. What arrangement did the English and German soldiers reach?
5. How did they celebrate Christmas?
6. Why did more of the Germans know English?
7. What help did one of the German soldiers ask from an English soldier?

Life Skills and Values

brotherhood, humanity

21ST CENTURY Critical Thinking

1. What lesson did you learn from the play? What do you think the old German soldier meant when he said that the answer lay in 'our hearts'?
2. How is this play relevant in today's world? Give examples to support your answer.

Vocabulary

contextual usage

ia **A. Fill in the blanks with these words from the story.**

frost exchange curious beaten souvenirs tinged

1. The ________________ boy hid in the shadows and listened to the two strangers talking.
2. The temperature dipped last night and the windows were covered in ________________.
3. Shaheen and I usually ________________ our notes while preparing for the exams.
4. The victorious team was consoling the players of the team they had ________________.
5. The sky was ________________ with the golden colours of the setting sun.
6. It was an empty stretch of the beach, with only a tiny shop selling ________________.

idioms related to the army

ia **B. Match these idioms related to the army with their meanings.**

Idiom	Meaning
1. on the double	a. very quickly, immediately
2. watch your back	b. (of a group) work closely together to defend themselves in a difficult situation
3. close ranks	c. be careful
4. in the trenches	d. in the most active and difficult parts of a job or business

C. Fill in the blanks with the idioms from the previous exercise. You may have to make some changes.

1. The pickpocket made for the train exit ________________ as soon as he realised that he had been spotted.
2. The officers would always ________________ around their own, and try to make excuses for their actions.
3. The senior journalist recalled his days ________________ at the start of his career, when he had to wait all day for meetings with important people.
4. The bowler better ________________. He has been warned twice by the umpire.

Grammar

types of sentences

You know that sentences are of four types.

An **assertive sentence** states something or provides some information. It can be positive or negative.

Example: It is 2:00 in the morning and most of our men are asleep in their dugouts.

An **interrogative sentence** asks a question. It can be a *wh-* question or a *yes/no* question.

Example: Why cannot we have peace and all go home?

An **imperative sentence** gives a command, an instruction, a piece of advice, or makes a request.

Example: You come over here.

An **exclamatory sentence** expresses strong emotions or feelings of excitement, joy, surprise, anger or sadness. It ends with an exclamation mark. (!)

Example: One of our lads walked off with the infamous spiked helmet!

Assertive sentences can be changed to interrogative and exclamatory sentences and vice versa.

Look at the table to understand how one type of sentence can be written as another.

Assertive	Interrogative	Exclamatory
It has been a terrible waiting.	Has it been a terrible waiting?	What a terrible waiting it has been!
We can't have peace and all go home.	Why can't we have peace and all go home?	Alas! We can't have peace and all go home!

ia **A. Rewrite the sentences as directed.**

1. Are we going to the book fair on Saturday? (Begin with: We are ...)
2. How charming you look in this hat! (Begin with: You look so ...)
3. This is quite a silly excuse. (Begin with: What a silly ...)
4. It is very hot in Delhi. (Begin with: How hot it ...)
5. Have they lost the battle? (Begin with: They have ...)
6. The mountains look so majestic. (Begin with: How majestic the ...)

prepositions of time and place

A **preposition** is a word or a group of words that shows the relationship of a noun, pronoun, or phrase with another word in a sentence. Some common prepositions are *in, at, on, of, to, by* and *with.*

Prepositions of time indicate time and duration.

Examples: It is 2 a.m. **in** the morning and most of our men are asleep in their dugouts.
We have agreed that there will be no shooting **till** midnight tomorrow.

Prepositions of place tell us where something is located with reference to another thing.

Examples: A new recruit got his feet stuck **in** the trap.
Lying **on** my cot, I must have drifted off to sleep.

ia **B. Fill in the blanks using suitable prepositions.**

1. The train leaves tomorrow ______ 8 o'clock ______ the morning.
2. Everyone gathered ______ midnight to celebrate Gairika'a birthday.
3. I take extra classes for mathematics ______ my school ______ two hours every Monday and Friday.
4. We decided to meet ______ the restaurant ______ 30 minutes.
5. I finished high school ______ 2023.
6. The audience was asked to be seated ______ the auditorium 15 minutes ______ the play began.

Study Skills

Pronunciation

words with silent consonants

Read these words aloud.

knapsack **w**ist lis**t**en Chris**t**mas **h**onour

You will notice that the highlighted consonants are silent when the words are pronounced.

Listen to the list of words and circle the silent consonant.

1. doubt
2. half
3. knee
4. wrong
5. ballet
6. gnome
7. honesty
8. yacht

Listening

listening for details

Listen to a passage on Florence Nightingale and fill in the blanks.

1. Florence was born into a wealthy ________________ family.
2. She always showed a deep interest in ________________ and caring for those ________________ than herself.
3. In those days nursing was considered a profession fit for the ________________.
4. Wounded soldiers were dying from ________________ rather than ________________.
5. Florence and her team started ________________ the hospital.
6. Florence would walk at night with a ________________, and the soldiers would call her ________________.

Speaking

narrating a chain story

A chain story is one in which each section or line is written by a different person, picking up from where the previous one left off. Work in groups and narrate a chain story on the topic 'a Christmas gift to remember', with each student narrating one line of the story. Remember that you have to link your sentence to what has happened before while being imaginative in adding new details.

You can use the following points for your story:

- the surprise of an unexpected gift
- something that you had been secretly hoping for or something strange and funny
- feeling of thankfulness/mystery surrounding the giver of the gift
- opening the gift, followed by Christmas cheer all around

Writing

diary entry

Imagine that you are a soldier stationed in the German trenches, who has just returned after spending Christmas with the English soldiers. Write a diary entry about the events that took place in no-man's-land on the Christmas of 1914.

You may use these points:

- how you and your fellow soldiers put out Christmas trees and sang carols
- the heart-warming reaction of the English soldiers
- how Christmas brought people close, erasing all borders
- your longing that the war would end soon so that you can return home

You may use the given format for your diary entry.

_______________ (Place)

_______________ (Date)

_______________ (Day of the week, time)

Dear Diary,

____

____

____

____

____

____

____

____

____

____

____

_______________ (Name of the writer)

Explore More

Read the book *The Enemy: A Book About Peace* by Davide Calì and Serge Bloch. It is about two soldiers who realize that both of them are people with family, friends and dreams, not just the enemy.

Watch the 1995 film *The Little Princess* directed by Alfonso Cuarón. It is about a young girl who is sent to a boarding school when her father leaves to fight in a war.

Listen to the song 'Imagine' by John Lennon about a peaceful world where people are not divided by war and borders.

humour

16

This Morning is Our History Test

Kenn Nesbitt

Curricular Goals

- explore the structure of poetry and literary devices
- writes about ideas and experiences for the purpose intended

Competencies

- can recognize rhyming couplets
- can interpret data presented in graphic form and answer questions

Reading

a *Do you think it is right to cheat? What would you do if you noticed a classmate cheating during an exam? Read this humorous poem about a student who has made preparations to cheat on his history test.*

This morning is our history test.
I've pinned my notes inside my **vest.**
Inside my coat I wrote my notes,
including dates and famous quotes.
I've written more upon my hand
that only I can understand,
and in my socks and sleeves I **stowed**[1]
my scribbled notes in secret **code.**

I've written down so many names
of winners of Olympic games,
of buildings, people, places too,
from **Tennessee** to **Timbuktu.**
I even copied down a piece
on **ancient** Rome and ancient Greece,
plus everything from **Shakespeare**'s plays
to who invented **mayonnaise.**

What were the various places where the student hid his notes?

Literary term

1. This is an example of **alliteration.** The words *socks, sleeves* and *stowed* begin with the 's' sound and are placed close together.

vest: a piece of clothing worn under a shirt
stowed: put carefully until needed
code: a system of words, letters, numbers or symbols that records information secretly or in a shorter form
Tennessee: a state in the southern part of the USA
Timbuktu: a city in Mali, Africa. It signifies any faraway place
ancient: very old or existing in a long time ago
Shakespeare: a famous sixteenth century English playwright and poet
mayonnaise: a thick, creamy sauce made from eggs, oil and vinegar, used in sandwiches and salads

I came to school so well prepared.
I wasn't nervous, wasn't scared.
But here it is, the history test.
I look inside my coat and vest
to get the dates and famous quotes
and find I cannot read my notes.
So much for Shakespeare, Greece and Rome.
I left my glasses back at home.

Cross-curricular Corner

The Olympic Games originated in ancient Greece. They were held as part of a religious festival to honour Zeus, the father of all gods and goddesses in Greek mythology.

Ancient Greece and Rome were key historical centres of culture and civilization in Europe.

In a Nutshell

Who a student

What cheating on a history test

Where in school

About the poet

Kenn Nesbitt (born in 1962) is an American children's poet. Some of his well-loved poems are 'My Dog Does my Homework ' and 'The Tale of the Sun and the Moon'.

Understanding the Poem

HOTS

ia **A. Choose the correct answer.**

1. Which of these lines does not use alliteration?
   a. 'from Tennessee to Timbuktu'
   b. 'on ancient Rome and ancient Greece'
   c. 'of buildings, people, places too'
2. What does the word 'Timbuktu' mean in the poem?
   a. a town in central Mali, West Africa
   b. a faraway place
   c. a state in the United States of America
3. What does the student mean by 'well prepared'?
   a. He read the lessons thoroughly.
   b. He has all the notes to cheat from.
   c. He is confident about the test.
4. Why couldn't he cheat in the end?
   a. He felt guilty.
   b. He forgot to bring his notes.
   c. He forgot his glasses at home.
5. What does the line 'So much for Shakespeare, Greece and Rome' mean?
   a. Shakespeare, Greece and Rome were not important in history.
   b. All the effort made to prepare the notes had gone to waste.
   c. Shakespeare, Greece and Rome were some of the most important topics in history.

6. What lessons do you learn from the poem? (You can choose more than one option.)
   a. If we try to take shortcuts instead of working hard, we may land in trouble unexpectedly.
   b. It is wrong to cheat.
   c. We should plan carefully in order to avoid mistakes.

B. Answer these questions in a few lines.

1. 'And in my socks and sleeves I stowed / my scribbled notes in secret code.' What does 'secret code' mean here? Explain these lines.
2. What were the things which the student copied?
3. The poem has an unexpected ending, or a 'twist in the tale'. What is it?

Life Skills and Values

planning, honesty

21ST CENTURY Flexibility | 21ST CENTURY Critical Thinking

1. The poem tells us about the last-minute preparations of a student before a test. How do you think the student in the poem could have prevented this situation?
2. Many students struggle with fear of tests and exams. Why do you think this is so?

Vocabulary

rhyming couplets

Read these lines and study the pattern of the rhyme scheme in the table.

This morning is our history <u>test</u>.
I've pinned my notes inside my <u>vest</u>.
Inside my coat I wrote my <u>notes</u>,
including dates and famous <u>quotes</u>.

test	*a*
vest	*a*
notes	*b*
quotes	*b*

The rhyme scheme of the stanza is *aabb*. This means that the first two lines, and the third and fourth lines rhyme with each other. Each pair thus forms a rhyming couplet.

A **rhyming couplet** is made up of two lines which rhyme with each other. The two lines together usually form a complete thought or idea.

A. Identify two other rhyming couplets from the poem and underline the rhyming words.

ia **B. Read the following stanza from the poem, 'The Duck and the Kangaroo' by Edward Lear. Circle the rhyming words and identify the rhyme scheme. Then, underline each rhyming couplet. How many are there in this stanza?**

'Please give me a ride on your back!'
    Said the Duck to the Kangaroo.
'I would sit quite still, and say nothing but "Quack,"
    The whole of the long day through!
And we'd go to the Dee, and the Jelly Bo Lee,

Over the land, and over the sea; –
    Please take me a ride! O do!'
    Said the Duck to the Kangaroo.

Activity

data interpretation

A **graph** is a diagram through which we can represent information on the relationship between two or more sets of numbers.

The following graph tells us how many Class 6 students in a school took part in dance, music and drama events in the annual concert.

The class is divided into four sections and the graph gives us information on their participation in each activity.

Study the graph and answer the questions that follow.

Annual Concert Participation of Class 6

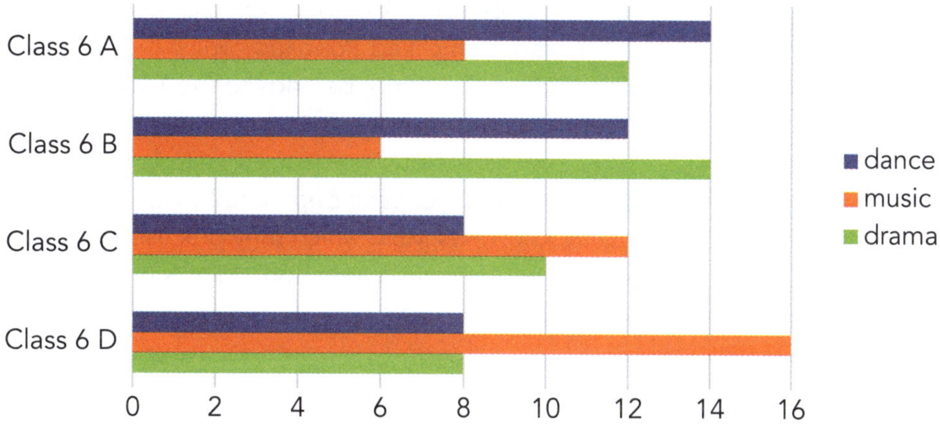

1. Which class has the highest student participation in music? __________
2. Which class has the highest participation in dance? __________
3. Which class has the lowest student participation in drama? __________
4. What is the total number of students in drama? __________
5. Which two classes have an equal number of students in dance? __________

Explore More

Read the book *Quirky History: The Swan Car of Nabha and Other Unusual Stories from History* by Mini Menon. It is a collection of strange but true events from Indian history.

Watch the 1988 TV series, *Bharat Ek Khoj*, by Shyam Benegal, about the 5000-year history of India, from ancient times to the present day.

UNIT IX

Overcoming Odds

Warm-up

A. Fill in the blanks with the given words to learn about the language and culture of the Lepcha people.

21ST CENTURY Information Literacy

agriculture mountain original staple languages Buddhism script

The Lepcha are one of the __________ peoples of Sikkim and Nepal, as well as parts of Bhutan, Tibet and the hills of West Bengal. They are also called *Rongkup*, which means 'beloved children of Rong'. The Lepcha tongue, called Róngring, belongs to the Tibeto-Burman group of __________. The Lepcha script, called *Róng*, was developed during the 17th and 18th centuries. It is based on the Tibetan __________. Lepcha society is organized into clans named after the __________ or lake which is sacred to them. Most Lepcha people follow __________. But they have also held on to their original faith, known as *Mun*, which they practise alongside Buddhism. Many practise __________, growing rice, oranges and cardamom. Rice is their __________ diet, along with wheat, maize and buckwheat.

B. One of the best ways to overcome odds in life is to persevere, or to continue trying and not give up. Work in pairs and find eight words in the grid related to the odds we face in life and the ways of overcoming them.

S	C	L	C	H	A	L	L	E	N	G	E	S	P	C
D	O	U	B	T	M	N	X	U	J	P	F	P	G	Z
E	U	N	Q	S	B	J	Y	Q	I	E	Y	F	C	M
S	R	R	J	H	K	O	R	N	H	Q	N	C	N	X
V	A	G	D	T	P	Y	R	D	T	Z	U	P	Z	O
W	G	C	O	N	F	I	D	E	N	C	E	Q	W	I
H	E	S	I	T	A	T	I	O	N	W	K	J	I	X
X	Q	K	S	D	X	E	N	P	V	V	E	Y	F	Z
N	S	A	C	H	I	E	V	E	M	E	N	T	K	G
Z	P	O	P	T	I	M	I	S	M	R	T	C	K	Z

17 non-fiction

Journey to a Lost Royal Lair

Anindya Mukherjee

Curricular Goals

- develop a comprehensive range of vocabulary in various contexts
- recognize basic linguistic aspects and use them in oral and written expression
- communicate effectively using language skills
- write about thoughts, feelings and experiences

Competencies

- can understand collocations and use one-word substitutes
- can use apostrophe to show possession
- can spell words with *au* sound
- can give a speech and write an article for the school magazine

Reading

a *Have you ever felt the urge to explore the unknown? Read a mountaineer's account of trekking through dense Himalayan forests in West Bengal to discover a long-lost royal hideout in the mountains.*

INDIA FOCUS

The Lepcha People

The Lepchas are one of the original peoples of Sikkim and Nepal. Tibetologist David Macdonald described the Lepchas as '... born **naturalist**[s] ... They know the habits of every beast and bird. [They] worship the spirits of mountain, forest, and river.'

In the Mahananda Wildlife Sanctuary in Darjeeling district lies the **fabled** *Raja Rani Pahar*. A veil of Lepcha **folklore** exists around it.

Raja Pahar from a distance

Raja Rani Pahar

In the mid-1990s, while participating in a survey by the West Bengal Forest Department on the Mahananda Wildlife Sanctuary, travel writer Heerak Nandy came across a local legend of the Lepchas that he mentioned in an article for a travel magazine. His article caught my interest, and with a small group of friends, I undertook an **exploratory** trip to *Raja-Rani Pahar* in 2001.

Stories in and around the village of Latpanchar, a tiny town in the Kurseong Hills, talk about the twin peaks of Raja and Rani, whose

What did the author come across in a travel magazine?

lair: hiding place

naturalist: a person who studies plants, animals, insects, and other living things

fabled: often talked about but rarely seen

folklore: stories and beliefs of a culture told by word of mouth

exploratory: done to examine something or find out more about it cliff faces are home to ancient caves and sacred symbols. These caves, said to be in the nearby Gulma Forest, are believed to have been the local Lepcha royals' hiding places during **invasions**.

Was there ever a Lepcha king or chieftain near the forest, I began to wonder. It turns out that Torve Pano, the first king of the Lepcha people, with his **royal seat** in Kurseong, did exist, with his reign believed to have been between 1400 and 1700 AD. There seemed to be a link between a **warring** Lepcha king and the folktale of a mysterious royal hideout near the capital of the same king.

Common idioms and phrases

1. **to go where angels dared not:** to go to a very wild and dangerous place

When I first began to investigate the Raja-Rani riddle in 2001, I was a wide-eyed young man in the fields of **mountaineering** and exploration. My wish to learn more about the unknown knew no limits, and I was ready to go where angels dared not[1]. I usually failed. Unsurprisingly, we couldn't locate the caves on the Raja-Rani peaks in 2001. But those setbacks didn't upset me.

Cross-curricular Corner

Elephant corridors are narrow natural paths that allow elephants to move between forests without being disturbed by humans.

I continued reading about the history, folklore and the geography of the area. Twenty-two years later, in 2023, it was time to return to find the caverns of Torve Pano. An expedition was born. I put together a team of six: Sukanta Deb Mandal, Subhajit Pal, Ashish Chanda, Rivu Soumya Das, Sourav Das and I. Aged between 29 and 52, the team combined the energy of youth with the wisdom and skill of experienced **outdoorsmen**. But above all else, my choice was based on how well each team member got along with the others.

The team, with the forest guides

invasions: acts of entering an area forcefully with an army
royal seat: place from where the king ruled
warring: fighting
mountaineering: activity of climbing mountains as a sport or hobby
outdoorsmen: people who spend a lot of time in outdoor activities, like camping, fishing

The Journey

On 11 February 2023, we reached Siliguri, a city in the foothills of the Himalayas. The next morning, we piled our luggage into a jeep and set off for Latpanchar town. Tall trees silently welcomed us as we left behind the **din and bustle** of Siliguri. These days, Latpanchar is a bird watcher's paradise and the greatest attraction for tourists is the rufous-necked hornbill. On 13 February, we started early for the jungle, accompanied by three forest guards. The trail was a sharp downhill and after about 1.5 kilometres, we reached a narrow **saddle**, which is an elephant corridor. Then the trail began to climb, at times, slowly, sometimes sharply. We took turns clearing a path, which was at times, completely hidden by vegetation, moving slowly and carefully.

Rufous-necked hornbill

Soon, we reached a **ridge** between the Raja and Rani peaks. Prayer flags adorned a few branches in a small clearing, which meant that **pilgrims** continue to visit the peaks today.

The steep walk downwards into the forest

We began our climb to the top of the Raja peak after a brief rest. There were times when we had to crawl beneath fallen tree trunks or wiggle through thorny **thickets**. We reached the top after about 700 metres of climbing. Raja peak's summit is very small. Hardly three or four people can sit side by side. Its southern end drops suddenly into emptiness below. The southerly wind brought back memories of 2001. I had had a **near-fatal** accident here then after a **free fall** down the cliff. But standing at the same spot now, I did not feel fear.

Onward we went, proceeding from Raja peak to Rani peak. At the top, we came upon some old coins and a ***trishul***. But we couldn't locate any

din and bustle: noise and hurried movement
saddle: (here) a low land between two highlands
ridge: a long narrow raised land with sloping sides formed by two sides of a mountain
pilgrims: people who journey to a sacred place for religious purposes
thickets: thick groups of smalls trees, shrubs, and similar plants
near-fatal: almost causing death
free fall: falling fast and uncontrollably
trishul: a three-pronged spear

caves along the cliff. We returned to our camp soon after and decided to devote our time and energy to finding the caves on Raja peak.

After exploring the area thoroughly and figuring out a trail, we returned to the top of Raja peak on 14 February. After two days of exhausting exploration, including going down the mountain's steep sides many, many times using a rope, we found that the cave, hidden under an **overhanging** rock face.

The Discovery

We returned on 16 February. We had planned to climb and enter the cave that day. Our excitement levels were at an all-time high as the **crucial** moment drew near. I soon found myself **dangling** mid-air in front of the cave we had worked so hard to reach. What followed was nearly an hour of **cliffhanger**-style action. I was almost 10 feet away from the cave. Swinging along its side like a **pendulum**, I made it inside the royal hideout after several tries.

The cave appeared to be nothing special at first – just a **hollow** in the rock wall. I discovered, however, that it could easily fit three to four people. About four feet away, we discovered a second cave that was wider and shallower than the first. Sneaking inside, I found that three people could fit there as well. Both the caves were dry and hidden from view from the ground below.

These caves, entered by people probably for the first time in centuries, were perfect emergency hideouts for the royal family during battles. The Lepcha people were masters of the forest and may have had rope ladders to reach the twin caves in times of emergency.

We were a happy group on 17 February, as we gathered our belongings and set out for the plains. Our team had

overhanging: sticking out over and above something
crucial: very important
dangling: swinging loose
cliffhanger: a dramatic and exciting moment in a story where you can't guess what will happen next; here, also literally hanging from the side of the cliff
pendulum: (in a clock) long straight part with a weight at the end, that moves regularly from side to side
hollow: having a hole or empty space inside

The first sighting of a cave, as a team member swings to reach it

The climber tries to pull himself inside the cave.

been blessed to serve as a **vessel** to rediscover the fabled caves, the Lepcha royal family's lost lair.

The discovery perhaps takes us back to a forgotten chapter in the history of the Lepchas. Investigations by experts can shed more light[3] on both the history and geography of the area, including the unusual shape of the caves high up in the mountains.

Common idioms and phrase

3. **to shed light:** This idiom means to reveal or explain something.

vessel: a person regarded as a medium or agent for some purpose a

In a Nutshell

- **Who** the author, Anindya Mukherjee
- **What** expeditions to find the lost Lepcha royal caves
- **Where** Raja-Rani Hills, Latpanchar
- **When** in 2023

About the author

Anindya Mukherjee (born 1971) is a mountaineer, explorer and writer from West Bengal. He has climbed mountain ranges across the world, including Nanda Devi East and the Zemu Gap in the Himalayas. He has cycled across Africa twice and retraced the original journey of Netaji Subhas Chandra Bose's Indian National Army from Singapore to Manipur.

Comprehension

HOTS

A. Arrange the sentences in the order of events in the story.

- ☐ The southerly wind on top of Raja peak reminded the author of his near-fatal accident in 2001.
- ☐ The author put together a team of six to go on the expedition to find the caves.
- ☐ The team returned to Raja peak on 14 February.
- ☐ At the top of Rani peak, they found some old coins and a *trishul* but no caves.
- ☐ The author read Heerak Nandy's article.
- ☐ The team members piled their luggage into a jeep and set out for Latpanchar town.

B. Answer the questions as directed.

1. Tibetologist David Macdonald said that the Lepchas of the time were 'born naturalists'. What did he mean?
   a. They were interested in studying zoology and botany.
   b. They knew the habits of every beast and bird.
   c. They were worshippers of natural resources.

2. *His article caught my interest, and with a small group of friends, I undertook an exploratory trip to Raja-Rani Pahar in 2001.*
   Which quality of the writer does this line show?
   a. that he acted without thinking   b. his outgoing nature   c. his love for adventure
3. Why do you think the Lepcha royals' hideout was so difficult to find and reach?
   a. The hideout was meant for protection and safety from enemies.
   b. The hideout also contained a secret treasure.
   c. It had not been visited by anyone in centuries, so everyone forgot about its location.
4. *Swinging like a pendulum, I made it inside the royal hideout after several tries.*
   Tick the literary device used in this sentence.
   a. personification   b. metaphor   c. simile
5. Write the reasons for the given actions.

Action	Reason
1. The team often had to clear a path through the forest and move slowly and carefully.	
2. The team was happy as they came down to the plains on 17 February.	

C. Answer the questions in a few lines.

1. What does the folklore in and around Latpanchar say?
2. What did the author find out about Torve Pano and the lost caves?
3. How do we know that pilgrims still visit the peaks?
4. 'What followed was nearly an hour of cliffhanger-style action.' Explain the two meanings of 'cliffhanger' here.
5. Describe the caves that the climbers found.

Life Skills and Values

perseverance, preparedness

21ST CENTURY Critical Thinking

1. The author faced failures and difficulties, but he did not give up and completed his expedition. What lesson do you learn from his story?
2. The expedition into the Himalayan forests required a lot of planning and preparation. Do you think that having a plan is important in our daily lives as well?

Vocabulary

collocations

A **collocation** is a group of two or more words that are often used together.

Examples: My choice was based on how well each team member **got along** with the others.
Tall trees silently welcomed us as we left behind the din and bustle of Siliguri.

ia **A. Match the words in Column A with those in Column B to form collocations. Then make sentences of your own with them.**

Column A	Column B
1. make	a. cold
2. pay	b. a secret
3. bitterly	c. exercise
4. keep	d. a wish
5. regular	e. attention

one-word substitutes

Many phrases can be replaced with a word which means the same.

Example: a high area of rock with a very steep side, often at the edge of the sea or ocean: **cliff**

ia **B. Choose the correct one-word substitutes for the given phrases.**

anonymous carnivores autobiography champion optimist

1. a person who is always hopeful and positive: ____________
2. written, given or made by somebody who does not want their name to be known: ____________
3. creatures who eat only meat: ____________
4. a person who performs the best at a particular skill or sport: ____________
5. a book about a person's life, written by him/her: ____________

Grammar

apostrophe to show possession

Read this sentence.

These caves have served as the Lepcha royals**'** hiding places. Here, the apostrophe (') after the word *royals* shows the relation between the *royals* and the *hiding places.*

An **apostrophe (')** is used to show that someone or something belongs or relates to someone or something else.

For plural nouns that already end in *s*, we add only the apostrophe (').

Example: They went out to search for him at his friends**'** houses.

We add an apostrophe *s* (*'s*) to plural nouns that do not end in *s*.

Example: Shyamal and his friends gathered at the children**'s** park.

ia Rewrite the sentences adding apostrophe (') or apostrophe *s* ('s) in the correct places.

1. My friends mother baked a cake for us.
2. There was a teachers meeting today.
3. Womens cricket has become popular in India.
4. The rabbits burrows are located deep in the woods.
5. The bearded man is Jacks uncle.
6. The butchers knife is very sharp.
7. The two teams performances were appreciated by everyone.

Study Skills

Spelling

words with *au* sound

Read these words aloud. Look at the different vowels and combination of vowels which all have the *au* sound.

b**o**rn   cr**aw**l   w**a**ll   exh**au**sting   ch**a**lk

Read the clues and write the words with *au* sound.

1. something that is uncooked ____________
2. to say something ____________
3. a white powder which we always add to food to make it taste better ____________
4. the hooked nail in a bird or an animal's feet ____________
5. the opposite of *tall* ____________
6. a place said to be inhabited by ghosts ____________

Listening

listening for information

Listen to a passage on the Lepchas and answer the questions.

1. What is the meaning of word 'lúngten'?
2. What does 'lúngten sung' mean?
3. What do the stories of the Lepchas tell us about?
4. What does the storyteller have to choose when telling a story?
5. What is the storytelling often influenced and spiced up with?

Speaking

giving a speech

A speech can influence people or convey information. A good speech should include the following:

- a strong **opening statement** that catches the audience's attention
- an **introduction** that presents the topic of the speech
- the **body** of the speech, including one or more ideas that stay with the audience. It can also include examples and facts related to the ideas.
- a **conclusion** that summarizes the main points

The writer faced many hurdles on his journey, but he did not lose heart. Give a speech of about 140–180 words in class on the topic 'overcoming challenges'.

21ST CENTURY Communication

You can include the following points:

- importance of determination and hard work, a positive attitude and willingness to learn
- staying focused on the goal
- an instance when you overcame a challenge

Useful words and phrases

- We often face difficulties in life...
- Just recently, I struggled with...
- But I have learnt that we should...
- I have realized that...

Writing

article in the school magazine

21ST CENTURY Initiative

Imagine that you went on a trekking holiday with your family during the summer vacation. You noticed during the trek that the trail was littered with plastic and other waste matter left behind by travellers. You collected and brought back some of the trash and also tried to educate fellow travellers along the way about the importance of keeping the mountains clean. Write an article of about 200 words for your school magazine about the experience. Give a short and catchy title to your article.

You can include the following points in your article:

- **Paragraph 1:** how littering affects the fragile environment of the mountains
- **Paragraph 2:** need to educate others about the problem
- **Paragraph 3:** what common people and the government can do to address the problem

Explore More

Read the travel book *Atlas of Adventures* by Lucy Letherland, which has illustrations about different cultures, people and wildlife from around the world.

Watch the 2005 documentary titled *Tingvong: A Lepcha Village in Sikkim* produced by the Namgyal Institute of Tibetology about the changes that the Lepcha people of the Dzongu reserve in North Sikkim have gone through in the last 75 years.

Listen to the song 'Fight Song' by Rachel Platten about the importance of small efforts in achieving our goals.

Answers to Warm-up on page 114:

A. 1. Diwali 2. Holi 3. Dussehra 4. Eid 5. Easter 6. Onam 7. Rakhi 8. Lohri

B. 1. Waldorf salad 2. Bombay duck 3. Chicken Chettinad 4. Bourbon biscuit 5. French toast 6. Turkish delight 7. Malabar parota 8. Black Forest cake didactic poem

18 A Psalm of Life

Henry Wadsworth Longfellow

Curricular Goals

- explore the structure of literary devices and forms of literature
- develop the ability to write about thoughts, feelings and experiences

Competencies

- can identify metaphors
- can write a short poem

Reading

a *What do you think your role in this world is? Do you feel that it is important for us to do something notable which will make people remember us in future? Read this poem which tells us how we can live a meaningful life.*

Tell me not, in **mournful** numbers,
Life is but an empty dream!—
For the soul is dead that **slumbers**,
And things are not what they seem.

Life is real! Life is **earnest**!
And the grave is not its goal;
Dust thou art, to dust returnest,
Was not spoken of the soul.

In the world's broad field of battle,
In the **bivouac** of life,
Be not like dumb, driven cattle!
Be a hero in the **strife**!

Lives of great men all remind us
We can make our lives **sublime**,
And, **departing**, leave behind us
Footprints on the sands of time[1];

Footprints, that perhaps another,
Sailing **o'er** life's **solemn main**,
A **forlorn** and shipwrecked brother,
Seeing, shall **take heart** again[2].

Let us, then, be up and doing,
With a heart for any fate;
Still achieving, still **pursuing**,
Learn to **labour** and to wait.

Literary terms

1. This is a **metaphor**, where the lasting effects of a person's achievements are compared to footprints people leave behind on a sandy beach.
2. This is a **metaphor**. Here, a person going through difficulties is compared to a shipwrecked sailor who finds hope in seeing the achievements of those who have come before him.

Cross-curricular Corner

Dust thou art, to dust returnest is a well-known phrase from *The Bible*. It means that the human body is created from the earth, and after death, becomes one with the earth again.

psalm: a song, poem or prayer that praises God
mournful: sad
slumbers: sleeps
earnest: serious
bivouac: temporary camp or shelter made and used especially by people climbing mountains or by soldiers
strife: fight
sublime: of very high quality, causing great admiration
departing: leaving
o'er: over
solemn: serious
main: (here) broad sea of life
forlorn: sad and lonely
take heart: find fresh courage
pursuing: following; (here) working towards a successful life
labour: work hard

In a Nutshell

What how to live a meaningful life in which we take our own decisions based on our wishes, rather than following what everyone else does

Why so our actions continue to make a difference in the lives of others long after we are gone

How by leading an active life, with an open heart that is ready to face any challenge

About the poet

Henry Wadsworth Longfellow (1807–1882) was a poet and novelist famous for works like *The Song of Hiawatha*, *Voices of the Night* and *Evangeline*. His poems were loved for their musical quality.

Understanding the Poem

ia HOTS

A. Choose the correct option.

1. What does the poet mean by the line, 'For the soul is dead that slumbers'?
   a. A person who is sleeping will not have new ideas.
   b. The mind of a person who doesn't think or have ideas of their own might as well be dead.
   c. Things are often not what they seem like in our dreams.
2. The line 'the grave is not its goal' means
   a. The goal of life is not just to live and die.
   b. Human beings should try to live as long as they can.
   c. Human beings should try not to live a boring life.
3. What does the world's 'broad field of battle' refer to?
   a. the difficulties we face in life
   b. the wars soldiers have to fight
   c. the shipwrecks which sailors have to deal with
4. What lesson do you learn from the poem?
   a. It is important to be the hero in every battle.
   b. We should do whatever we want in life.
   c. It is important to live a meaningful life in which people remember us for the good things we did.

B. Answer the questions in a few lines.

1. What do the lives of great men remind us?
2. What does the phrase 'take heart' mean? How can our actions help other people who are going through a difficult time?
3. What does the last stanza of the poem encourage us to do?

Life Skills and Values

positivity and strength

21ST CENTURY Critical Thinking

1. What are your hopes and dreams which you think will make your life meaningful and happy?
2. Does anything, or anyone inspire you to carry on when things seem difficult?

Vocabulary

metaphor

A **metaphor** is a figure of speech in which a person or a thing is compared to another, otherwise unrelated person or thing.

In a metaphor, the comparison is usually implied, and not directly stated using the words *as* or *like*, as is done in the case of a simile.

Example: Life is but an empty dream. (Life is being compared to a dream that has no meaning.)

ia **Read the passage carefully. Then, underline the metaphors and circle the similes.**

Breakfast on Sundays is like a movie production in my house. The sky is a blue umbrella by the time the breakfast table is laid. The sunbeams fall across the table like the stripes on a tiger's back. The aroma of good food floats around the house like a happy ghost inviting everyone to join in. Buttered pancakes are piled on a plate like a golden mountain. Mother, a goddess in the kitchen, hands out heaped plates of food to everybody.

Activity

writing a poem

21ST CENTURY Creativity

Look at the picture and write a short poem on it, on the theme 'dreams and hopes for the future'.

Useful words and phrases

rise	succeed
grow	aim
dream	effort
future	belief

Explore More

Read the poem 'The Character of the Happy Warrior' by William Wordsworth about an inspirational leader who continues to have enthusiasm for life, despite his responsibilities.

Watch the 2003 film *Finding Nemo* by Andrew Stanton about Marlin, the cowardly clownfish, rescuing his son, Nemo, when he gets kidnapped.

Project 3

A. In the chapter 'The Theft of the Ruby,' you read about some food traditions related to Christmas. These traditions vary from country to country.

Work in pairs and find out about food traditions related to festivals in any three countries of your choice. Make a collage with images and present it to the rest of the class. Remember to include the story behind each tradition too.

Information Literacy

Christmas food traditions

- Oysters in France
- Dried or salted fish in Norway
- Sweet rice pudding in the Philippines

bagless day activity

B. In 'Journey to a Lost Royal Lair' you read about the determination of a group of mountaineers as they trekked through mountainous forests to discover a long-forgotten hideout.

Productivity

1. **Watch the video *Kilimanjaro – The Summit* (https://vimeo.com/139758018) in class. The video captures the emotions of the mountaineers as they reach the top. In groups, discuss the following:**

- What seems both challenging or enjoyable about the experiences these people had?
- Why would someone want to risk their life to reach the top of a mountain?

> Kilimanjaro is one of the Seven Summits. These are the tallest mountains in each of the seven continents. The others are:
>
> - Denali, North America
> - Mount Aconcagua, South America
> - Mount Elbrus, Europe
> - Mount Vinson, Antarctica
> - Mount Everest, Asia
> - Mount Kosciuszko, Australia

2. **Find out about the Seven Summits. Divide the class into seven groups, with each group being assigned a summit.**
Research the following points for your summit:

- Height and country in which the peak is located
- Alternate names
- Interesting fact
- First climbed by

Make a presentation in class on mountaineering and the Seven Summits. Include the points that came up during your discussion on the reasons why people take up mountaineering.

Information Literacy